MOSES: GOD'S DELIVERER

COMPILED BY HAYES PRESS

Published by:

HAYES PRESS Publisher, Resources & Media

The Barn, Flaxlands

Royal Wootton Bassett

Swindon, SN4 8DY

United Kingdom

www.hayespress.org

I0200649

Table of Contents

CHAPTER ONE: EARLY LIFE AND FLIGHT (REG DARKE)

———

His birth was kept a secret, but his death was proclaimed publicly by God. He was born in captivity, but lived to be the world's greatest emancipator. He made no claim to oratory, but his words have left an indelible mark on his own nation and the nations at large. He is defamed by critics for the wrongs he did, but few will deny him the honour of being one of the greatest of the men of destiny. Who is this person, to whom the Almighty spoke audibly, and described with affection as "My servant"? He is none other than Moses, who was born in Egypt 3,500 years ago during a reign of terror; of an obscure family, yet from his birth he was ordained of God to be a mighty leader.

The greatness of this man was due to a quirk of fate, cry the sceptics! Not so, answers the Christian. It was due to the hand of God working in conjunction with the implicit faith of his parents. And the word of God throws its full weight behind the latter statement (Hebrews 11:23). The birth of Moses took place during a time of much fear and adversity. The children of Israel were slaves in Egypt, and for years they toiled, and suffered, and groaned under the malicious tyranny of Pharaoh and his ruthless officers (Exodus 1:8-20). Although the days were dark, and seemed to be growing darker for the people of God, out of some of the humble dwellings there radiated a light of faith and hope which heaven alone witnessed.

One such home belonged to Amram and Jochebed, the father and mother of Moses (Exodus 2:1). They might have been unaware of the divine interest shown in their marriage, their home, and their family; but the eye of God was certainly upon their house, and His hand was moving in it to begin a great work for Israel which was to involve their son Moses. We should pause here to comment on the importance the Lord attaches to Christian families. This is one avenue through which He works, and because of this the enemy is consistently busy trying to frustrate the divine plan. God's churches today are made up of individuals and families, and we must never lose sight of the importance of the home to God and His work. Luke reveals the great value of the family unit in the building up of the early churches of God. Lydia and the Philippian jailer are good examples of this (Acts 16); while Priscilla and Aquila lend added support by their work in the home with its remarkable results (Acts 18:1-3; 24-28). Further evidence can be found with Chloe and Stephanas (1 Corinthians 1:11,16), Philemon (vv.1,2), and the selected names on the honour roll of Romans 16. Today, there are children who are the fruit of much prayer and faithful testimony; they, in turn, will raise their children accordingly, and so perpetuate the divine testimony.

At a time when Egypt's king had decreed that every male child born to Israelites was to be murdered at birth (Exodus 1:16,22), to Amram and Jochebed, a faithful, fearless couple of the tribe of Levi, a son was born. They had learned the secret of not doubting in the darkness what God had revealed to them in the light. Hundreds of years later this striking tribute is paid to them by the writer of the Hebrews epistle: "By faith Moses, when he was born, was hid three months by his parents ... and they were not afraid of the king's commandment" (Hebrews 11:23). Stephen says that the baby Moses was "exceeding fair" (fair unto God); and he was nourished three months in his father's house (Acts 7:20).

These were three anxious months, no doubt, as the parents sought to protect in the home the secret of the birth of this "goodly child" (Hebrews 11:23), yet the faith of Amram and Jochebed never wavered. But a crisis was building up, quite possibly due to house-to-house searches on the part of Pharaoh's soldiers for Israeli baby boys, and Jochebed was forced to provide a place of refuge for her unnamed son. Diligent, skilful fingers moved rapidly as she wove tightly the papyrus rushes into an ark; a place of protection for Israel's future leader, who was to live a full and significant life span of 120 years. This, to all intents and purposes, appeared to be divided into three equal parts. Forty years were spent by Moses in Egypt learning to be something; forty years in the desert learning he was nothing; and forty years with the children of Israel learning that God is everything.

The completion of the sleeping basket, with its insulating barriers of slime and pitch set in motion a dramatic sequence of events. There would be great excitement in the home as the baby was swaddled in suitable clothing, and placed in the basket; and no doubt, moments of solemnity would follow as the family secret would be commended to Jehovah with the prayer of faith and love. Then father or mother would steal quietly away, perhaps in the darkness, to the pre-chosen spot on the banks of the Nile where seclusion could be found amidst the thickly growing reeds.

"The night has a thousand eyes", a poet has said, but above all others would be the eye of God, observing from the light of heaven, every movement in this human drama. The family guardian of the babe in the bulrushes was his sister Miriam, the very one who would later lead the happy women of Israel to respond with song and timbrel to the triumphant words of Moses' song of deliverance after the nation came dry-shod through the Red Sea (Exodus 15:20,21). "She stood afar off", but with a roving, protective eye, she would be alert to any dangers involving her young brother. We are not told how long Miriam kept vigil, but it ended when, as she bathed in the river, Pharaoh's daughter saw the ark among the reeds. When the basket was opened a weeping babe was found within. In the event which followed we see again the wonderful hand of God at work, guiding through all the complications and circumstances with unerring care and wisdom.

What a lesson is to be learned by us from this! How anxious, fearful, and even panic-stricken we might have been in such a situation, even to hindering God's purpose! How prevailing faith can be when we quietly trust and are not afraid (Psalm 56:3)! In view of the enmity and fear prevalent in Egypt towards the Israelite, one would have expected the princess to show anger when she cried, "This is one of the Hebrews' children" (v.6); but instead she showed compassion. This, coupled with the bravery of Miriam, who boldly suggested that she call a Hebrew nurse, resulted in Jochebed arriving on the scene to be given the task of nursing her own child, and being paid for it!

It would be a day of great rejoicing in the Levitical home when the youngest was returned to the bosom of the family so unexpectedly. Our hearts should rejoice, too, as we see the quiet, yet positive way, that God forges link after link in the lives of individuals, to produce a chain of testimony to His unlimited care, protection, and interest. The midwife, the mother, and the sister, all played their part under God, without being aware of the divine plan which was centred in the boy. Years later, perhaps, they would have an opportunity to view it all in retrospect, and be encouraged at being chosen as God's co-workers. The Lord is, indeed, "over all, blessed for ever. Amen" (Romans 9:5).

Although it is not revealed how long Jochebed was allowed to nurse her son, we can be sure that he prospered in body, soul, and spirit under her nourishing care. But her emotions would be very mixed on the day she journeyed to the palace to hand over the child to the princess. Hidden grief and restrained tears would be needful as the daughter of Pharaoh acclaimed the child as her own. "... and he became her son. And she called his name Moses, and said, "Because I drew him out of the water" (2:10), a Hebrew child with an Egyptian name, which was never changed, not even by God. The Lord changed the names of Abram and Jacob, but not of Moses. Perhaps He wanted the name to be a perpetual reminder to Moses that his deliverance and protection were symbolic of what was done for Israel.

Some might consider it a golden opportunity to grow up as a son in the palace of a mighty ruler, but these remarkable words are written about this period in Moses' life: "By faith Moses, when he was grown up, refused to be called the son of Pharaoh's daughter; choosing rather to be evil entreated with the people of God, than to enjoy the pleasures of sin for a season; accounting the reproach of Christ greater riches than the treasures of Egypt; for he looked unto the recompense of reward" (Hebrews 11:24-26).

Moses would be exposed to all the opportunities of political knowledge, worldly education, military training, and entertainment, in Egypt; and there is no doubt that he was well versed in mathematics, astronomy, hieroglyphics, magical arts, and the philosophies. He "was instructed in all the wisdom of the Egyptians; and he was mighty in his words and works", Stephen tells us (Acts 7:22). He was a worthy successor to Joseph, who was Egypt's saviour in a former generation, but Moses sacrificed the fame and treasures of Egypt when he decided to identify himself with his own people. "Choosing rather to be evil entreated" indicates that he was well aware of the consequences and the reactions of the Egyptians, when he paid that first memorable visit to the downtrodden Israelites. He wanted to share the burden of his brethren, and to help them in their sorrow. He was in the prime of life, almost forty years old, when "it came into his heart to visit his brethren" (Acts 7:23). What he found was not pleasant as he looked on their distress and bitterness. When he saw an Egyptian striking a Hebrew "he looked this way and that way", before killing the Egyptian and burying him in the sand (Exodus 2:11,12).

Moses was yet to learn that "looking up" should precede drastic actions and deeds of importance; that his instructions must come from the Eternal God whose dwelling place he found to be a refuge (Psalm 90:1). Moses had good intentions, but he could not help Israel on his own. He had to be prepared by God and sent by Him. The same hand which struck the Egyptian in anger, would also strike the rock in error, and Moses would be denied the privilege of leading Israel into the land. "The flesh profiteth nothing", said the Christ (John 6:63), whose reproach Moses would count of greater riches than the treasures of Egypt. The Lord Jesus came from the "ivory palaces, into a world of woe" to accomplish a work far greater than that of Moses. He also identified Himself with His brethren; He saw their burdens and sorrows and became acquainted with their grief (Isaiah 53); He had compassion on them (Mark 6:34), and gave His life as a sacrifice in order to bring salvation and deliverance to Israel and the whole world.

Addressing the Jews of his day, Stephen presents the point of view that Moses defended and avenged the Israelite attacked by the Egyptian; "And he supposed that his brethren understood how that God by his hand was giving them deliverance; but they understood not" (Acts 7:24-26). The following day Moses' problem was compounded when he visited his brethren a second time and tried to act as mediator between two of them engaged in an argument. One of them thrust him away saying, "'Who made you a ruler and a judge over us? Do you want to kill me as you did the Egyptian yesterday?" (vv.27,28 NKJV). Fear gripped the heart of Moses, and Pharaoh, hearing of the incident, sought to kill him. Moses fled for his life from

Egypt into the land of Midian where he remained forty years as a shepherd until the Lord appeared unto him at the burning bush, and prepared him for the task of returning to Egypt (Acts 7:29,30).

Moses' moment of fear must not be misconstrued, for the Spirit makes it clear that "By faith he forsook Egypt, not fearing the wrath of the king; for he endured, as seeing Him who is invisible" (Hebrews 11:27). It was the same faith which enabled him to return to Egypt, where he was welcomed by his people, and he proved his credentials by his words and works. In this we see him again as a type of Messiah who will return a second time to earth, and be welcomed as the rain (Hosea 6:3), and will rule among His people. Moses may have failed in his early attempts at deliverance and mediation, but God enabled him to return to Egypt with a shepherd's rod - something despised by the Egyptians (Genesis 46:34) - to emancipate a people later called holy by Him; and when they failed, God allowed him to mediate on their behalf, and he was successful with God. The pleadings of Moses on this grave occasion give us an insight into the true character of the man called by God, "My servant".

CHAPTER TWO: AT THE BURNING BUSH (TOM HYLAND)

―――――

From the splendour and affluence of the Egyptian court to the solitude and privation of the desert from the high affairs of state for which he had been carefully groomed to the menial duties of an eastern shepherd; such was the sudden, dramatic turnabout in the life of Moses, the man destined to fill a key place in God's dealings with mankind.

Yet this unforeseen episode was to play a vital part in the preparation of the chosen vessel. When he fled from Egypt Moses was "mighty in his words and works", but he was not yet ready for the momentous undertaking to which God was training him. Forty years of exile in the wilderness were necessary to balance his character and mature his talents. The impetuosity of early manhood must be tempered by adversity and self-discipline. In the palace he had been "instructed in all the wisdom of the Egyptians". In the desert he was to be fashioned in the school of God until the cultured statesman became "meek, above all the men which were upon the face of the earth". The process was prolonged and severe: the finished product was unique. Now Moses was ready for the high office he was destined to fill, and the call to service came with the same dramatic suddenness as the flight from Egypt forty years before.

A veil is drawn over those solitary wilderness years. Moses would have ample opportunity for reflection. The bitter memory of rejection by his brethren persisted, but there were no regrets for the choice he made. He refused to be called the son of Pharaoh's daughter, not from necessity but from calm and deliberate choice. No longer could he be at home in the palace while his brethren languished in slavery. But they had refused him, misunderstood his concern for them, and endangered his life by their callous conduct. What news reached him of the fortunes of his brethren during his exile is not disclosed. Had he plans to return to Egypt or did he expect to live out his days in obscurity? We do not know. But he knew the terms of the Abrahamic covenant and the glorious destiny of his people. As the future historian of that patriarchal age, Moses was aware that emancipation was near (Genesis 15:13,14). But he was far away from the hub of events, and it does not appear that he had an inkling that he was to be the chosen leader.

The Red Sea and a great and terrible wilderness lay between the children of Israel and the land of promise. A man of God was at hand with all the necessary qualifications, including an unrivalled knowledge of wilderness conditions acquired through forty years of practical experience. Meanwhile, the children of Israel grew and multiplied in Egypt. As their condition became more desperate, no one could foresee how the promise of God would be implemented. But "God moves in a mysterious way His wonders to perform."

In every age God employs human instruments to carry out His great designs. The preparation goes on in secret. Whether the form of service be small or great by human standards does not matter; His hand shapes the vessel until it is "fit for the Master's use". He decides where, when and how the vessel will be used. One of the great lessons to be learned from His plan for Moses is the wisdom of submission to His overruling hand in the ups and downs of our lives. God may lead in unexpected ways. He can even use our mistakes to train us for future service. Although we may be unable to discern His purpose in the setbacks and reverses we encounter:

"The dark threads are as needful,

In the Weaver's skilful hand,

As the threads of gold and silver

In the pattern He has planned."

The life of a wilderness shepherd was austere and hazardous. It demanded endurance and skill of a high order. There was a familiar sameness in the daily routine but the shepherd always had to be on the alert for the unexpected. No doubt Moses had often led Jethro's flock through the awesome shadows of Mount Horeb. A wilderness bush on fire would not be an extraordinary sight. But on this day of destiny his trained eye observed a bush-fire which was different from any other he had seen. This bush did not quickly subside when the flames enveloped it. As it burned it remained erect and intact. This was a "great sight", and Moses approached to investigate. Then came the voice the Voice of God: "Moses, Moses, ... draw not nigh hither". A solemn, unforgettable moment - God was here. In a flash this ordinary working day in the wilderness was transformed to become the crucial day in the life of Moses. It happens like this with many of God's servants. The call to service comes suddenly, unexpectedly, with compelling power. Moses waited barefooted until the silence of the desert was again broken as the Voice announced: "I am the God of thy father, the God of Abraham, the God of Isaac, and the God of Jacob" (Exodus 3:6).

The Speaker had now identified Himself in covenant terms, and as Moses hid his face from the fearful splendour of the divine presence the Voice continued: "I have surely seen the affliction of My people which are in Egypt, and have heard their cry by reason of their taskmasters; for I know their sorrows; and I am come down to deliver them out of the hand of the Egyptians, and to bring them up out of that land unto a good land and a large, unto a land flowing with milk and honey; unto the place of the Canaanite (vv.7,8).

Moses listened, enthralled. From childhood days he had pondered the terms of God's covenant with Abraham. In accordance with that covenant a period of four hundred years was to elapse before the promised seed would be ready to possess their inheritance (Genesis 15:13). In those intervening years God was preparing the children of Israel for nationhood. Their period of bondage in Egypt was an important element in that preparation. Now He is moving forward to the next stage which was a decisive development for Israel and for mankind. Moses is given confirmation that the time of emancipation has arrived - God has come down to deliver.

Whatever ideas he had before as to how the terms of the covenant would be implemented Moses must have been staggered by the magnitude of the plan spelled out to him there at the Burning Bush. Not only would this vast company of men, women and children be delivered from their bondage and leave the land of Egypt with all their belongings; they would also have to trek across that arid wilderness to the land of promise. None better than Moses could assess the perils of such an undertaking and the enormous problems which would have to be resolved. Moreover, Pharaoh would need to be persuaded to release his captives. Moses knew that all the cunning of that ruthless tyrant would be employed to thwart any attempt to free them from his power. But no sooner had the plan been announced to Moses than the divine arrangement for its execution was disclosed: "Come now, therefore, and I will send you to Pharaoh that you may bring My people, the children of Israel, out of Egypt" (Exodus 3:10 NKJV).

No one who is truly called to serve God feels competent for the task. And Moses was no exception. His reaction was the normal response of a humble-minded man. Self-distrust is not cowardice. It might be argued that the Lord's, "I will send you", was sufficient, and that Moses should have accepted without question the commission assigned to him. But we have an infinitely gracious God who bears gently with His servants, especially when the task allotted seems impossible by human calculation. The ensuing dialogue between Moses and God is on record for the encouragement of all His servants. It is not wrong to seek assurance and confirmation from God. We should bear in mind that this remarkable passage is among things "written aforetime for our learning". The record of God's dealings with men under the Old Covenant reveals the character and ways of our unchanging God.

Moses' self-deprecating plea, "Who am I, that I should go unto Pharaoh?" is offset by the pledge, "Certainly I will be with you". Not only do you have My authority, you will also have My presence; I will be at your side. Moses then expressed his fears that when he told his brethren in Egypt that the God of their fathers had sent him they would ask, "What is His Name?" Again, God allayed the fears of His servant by affirming to him the mystery of His eternal self-existence, in the sublime declaration, "I AM THAT I AM: ... Thus you shall say to the children of Israel, 'I AM has sent me to you". This divine formula expressing timelessness, immutability and infinity - incomprehensible to created beings - is embodied in the name JEHOVAH, the name by which He would now be known to His people, Israel - "This is My name for ever, and My memorial to all generations.

Assurance of the divine presence and disclosure of the divine name having been given, the Voice then proceeded to outline to Moses the course of action to be followed in the initial stages of his mission. He would go first to the elders of Israel with Jehovah's message and then to Pharaoh with Jehovah's demands. Still Moses demurred. No doubt the memory of his rejection by his brethren forty years before weighed heavily on his mind at this moment: "They will not believe me", he said. Once more God graciously accommodated His servant by giving him two miraculous evidential signs: the rod turned serpent and the hand turned leprous. And, as if to concede that his brethren would be difficult to convince, He gave instructions for a third sign to be used should this be necessary. He should take of the water of the river Nile, sacred to the Egyptians, pour it upon dry land, and the water would become blood. Surely no one would then question his credentials!

The bush still burns and the dialogue continues. There was yet another reservation in the mind of Moses as he reflects on the public prominence into which his mission would bring him. In the Egyptian court he had been a man of words, but for the past forty years his environment had been the great silences of the desert. Of his own choice he preferred obscurity to prominence. Like some other great men, he had learned to value the deep peace and tranquility of a pastoral life. He shrank from the bustle and strife his mission would entail - he preferred to continue his present mode of life. "Oh Lord", he said, "I am not eloquent ... for I am slow of speech, and of a slow tongue". Moses was now moving from a proper and understandable reluctance to the borderline of self-will.

The human mouth and powers of speech were the Creator's gift. As His chosen servant, Moses needed to be reminded that all his powers were expendable. His mouth and tongue had been set apart by Jehovah for His use in one of the great crises in human history. But even a further sharp reminder that he was under divine authority did not deter Moses from his final attempt to evade the high office for which God had fitted him: "O my Lord, please send by the hand of whomever else You may send," he pleaded (Exodus 4:13 NKJV).

Moses must now learn the important lesson that the unchangeable I AM, although patient and gracious, does not tolerate interference in the disposition of His servants. There is a finality about the last concession to Moses. Aaron, his elder brother, who was a good speaker, would be at his disposal as an intermediate spokesman. But Moses would be leader; Aaron would be subordinate. It remained for Moses to comply; his instructions are now complete. The interview is terminated, a man of God is enlisted to undertake the great work for which he had been prepared from the day of his birth eighty years before. The wilderness bush which had been the divine instrument reverts to its former state, but its story goes into inspired history for all time.

Moses for the last time guides the flock back to Jethro his father-in-law, pondering the events of that memorable day and conscious of the heavy burden which had been placed upon his shoulders. He had looked towards the end of his life; God had in view a new beginning. But the assurances he had received would be carefully reviewed and he would go forward in faith, and with "the good will of Him that dwelt in the bush" (Deuteronomy 33:16). And for the rest of his life, like that wilderness bush, he too would glow with holy fire and yet be unconsumed - he would dwell with God and speak with Him face to face.

CHAPTER THREE: THE HAND OF GOD (REG DARKE)

———

He was a refugee murderer when he stepped over the Egyptian border on his way to Midian. The hand that slew a man later enclosed itself around a shepherd's rod. This was a curious thing to do since the Egyptians were taught that shepherds were an abomination (1). Such was the beginning of the second forty-year era of Moses' life. In the land of his birth, Egypt, he became a man of affairs, a trained administrator, a capable handler of people. Yet he still lacked the essentials needed by a man who was to emancipate and lead a holy nation. So for forty years as a shepherd in Midian he was to learn dependence upon God, patience in service and tender care for the sheep and lambs of his flock. At the end of those years of training God spoke to him from the burning bush.

In preparation for this mammoth task God began with the eyes of Moses. The great power and glory of Egypt were etched on Moses' mind and vision, but they were nothing in comparison with the bush which burned and was not consumed. Moses was overwhelmed by this desert wonder. It exceeded everything he had ever seen before. This nation of destiny might pass through the fires of affliction, but He would see to it that she was not consumed. This great sight, this experience of God's holiness and power, was a turning point in the life of Moses. He would now see God and His purposes through new eyes, through sanctified vision.

The Lord next dealt with the hand which fatally struck a man. It held a shepherd's rod, for Moses cared for sheep in the wilderness. At God's command the rod was thrown to the ground where it changed to a serpent. Moses was commanded to pick it up by the tail and it became a rod in his hand again: a sanctified rod for divine service. What was learned here? That human ability at its best is not sufficient for God; that obedience to His commands is essential; that fear of the enemy, or his death-dealing sting, had been invalidated. Possessing a sanctified hand of obedience, Moses realized that God is stronger than His foes and the power of Egypt was not to be feared. Egypt is a type of the world, and today's Christian can draw a valid lesson from Moses' life.

The third experience for Moses was for the hand to be placed in his bosom, and on withdrawal it was found to be leprous. Indicated here is a truth for all to learn, that "in me, that is, in my flesh, dwelleth no good thing" (2). The "arm of flesh" must always fail despite our good intentions. The flesh is unclean, profitable for nothing, unacceptable to God. When the leprous hand was returned to the bosom and again taken out, it was clean. Now it could be used by God. Yet, with sanctified eyes and hand, Moses was still reluctant to serve God by returning to his former homeland, because he was not eloquent. He was commanded to go with the rod of His authority, and convey God's message via Aaron. Together they successfully confronted Egypt's despot which resulted ultimately in Israel's mighty deliverance from bondage (3).

But God was not finished with Moses yet. Israel was free, the Red Sea had been crossed, the covenant of obedience had been sealed by blood, the tabernacle was in process of being built' the law and commandments were written, and Moses sought yet another assurance. "Show me ... Your glory", he asked of the Lord. "You cannot see My face: for no man shall see Me, and live", answered the Lord. Then He made a startling suggestion, "Here is a place by Me, and you shall stand on the rock. So it shall be, while My glory passes by, that I will put you in the cleft of the rock, and will cover you with My hand while I pass by. Then I will take away My hand, and you shall see My back; but My face shall not be seen" (4).

We must picture Moses resting, relaxing, in the cleft of the rock so close to God, and joyously, assuredly, gazing at the hand of God. Surely the memory of this would linger with him all his days. He saw with assurance the hand of God in his life. It was the hand of the great Creator, the hand of the Deliverer, the hand of the supplier of the manna and the water from the rock. The unmistakable hand of God! Moses would look back in awe at the realization that nothing is accomplished for God unless His hand is in it.

And so today we need the same assurance of the hand of God in our lives. We must not be content with "getting by" in Christian experience, knowing only the rise and fall of uncertainty in our Christian walk. We must see and know that divine hand with its guidance and protection. He is willing to give us this faith experience which can regulate, stabilize our lives to make them fruitful. It will not only be a joy to us, but an encouragement to others to hear of the hand of God in one's life. With this experience there comes, too, the need for sanctified eyes to see God's purpose. Should we not pray on opening our Bibles, "Open my eyes, that I may see wondrous things from Your law" (5). Desiring, too, sanctified hands which hold aloft the rod of God, type of His authority which His Word reveals, that we may teach, reprove, correct, instruct, with righteousness in view. At the end of Moses' life God spoke of him as "My servant" (6). What of you and me? Our ideal is to rest in our service for Him, and see the hand of God.

(1) Genesis 46:34 (2) Romans 7:18 (3) Exodus 4:10-31 (4) Exodus 33:17-23 NJKV (5) Psalm 119:18 NKJV (6) Joshua 1:2

CHAPTER FOUR: MOSES AND PHAROAH (LAURIE BURROWS)

W hen Moses and Pharaoh first met, onlookers must have been impressed by the contrast between them: Moses, the meekest of men and Pharaoh, one of the worst tyrants the world has ever known. They were soon to realise, however, that with Moses was the power of God whereas Pharaoh's resources were but those of puny man. Although historians differ as to the identity of the king of Egypt at this time, there can be no doubt about his character for it is clearly portrayed in Scripture (Exodus 5-15).

He was quite a different type of man from the Pharaoh of Joseph's day; the king before whom Joseph stood quickly accepted the testimony of the exiled son of Jacob to the God of Israel observing, ""Can we find such a one as this, a man in whom is the Spirit of God?" Then Pharaoh said to Joseph, "Inasmuch as God has shown you all this, there is no one as discerning and wise as you" (Genesis 41:38, 39 NKJV). Later, this Pharaoh was pleased to receive the blessing of God from the hand of the aged Jacob and to do good to the children of Israel for the sake of Joseph whose work in saving Egypt from starvation he never forgot. Scripture clearly depicts him as an upright man who believed in God.

But in the course of time "there arose a new king over Egypt, which knew not Joseph" (Exodus 1:8). Rule had fallen into the hands of another dynasty of which nothing good is mentioned in the divine record. The first king of the new regime oppressed the Israelites and made them slaves, then he decreed that all their male infants should be drowned in the river Nile; but Moses, through the exemplary faith of his parents, escaped and was brought up in the palace. It seems likely that the Pharaoh from whom Moses fled at the age of forty, and his successor at the time of the Exodus, were also members of this dynasty, which was characteristically cruel to the Israelites. They all maintained the same system of heartless slavery, using forced labour to build cities for their own glorification. The story shows that the ruler whom Moses confronted to request the release of God's people was not a God-fearing man. He and his people were idol-worshippers (Exodus 12:12). He said ""Who is the Lord, that I should obey His voice to let Israel go? I do not know the Lord, nor will I let Israel go" (Exodus 5:2 NKJV).

Even when some of the Egyptians were persuaded to acknowledge the power of God on seeing the effects of the plagues (Exodus 8:19; 9:20; 10:7) Pharaoh refused to humble himself. Only under extreme pressure of circumstances did he ask Moses to entreat the Lord (Exodus 9:27,28; 10:16, 17), but he was insincere; as soon as each plague was withdrawn he changed his mind.

Such was the haughty and despotic ruler to whom Moses was sent on behalf of down-trodden Israel. Perhaps the Egyptian's cruel, unbending character was a byword among the nations round about. If so, it would in part explain Moses' initial hesitance at the burning bush to comply with the divine request to lead Israel out of Egypt. But eventually, accompanied by his brother Aaron, fresh from the slavery of the brickfields, Moses stood with shepherd's staff in hand in the court of the tyrant Pharaoh to demand the release of the people of God from Gentile slavery, and to deliver God's command, "Let My people go". To all appearances it was a most unequal confrontation. Pharaoh was disdainful: "Get you unto your burdens" he said, unaware that irresistible divine power was about to be exerted on behalf of the slaves. Although he ordered his taskmasters to intensify the Israelites' burdens and was prepared to marshal his armed forces for battle, such things could not dismay Moses who was daily instructed in every detail of the campaign by his divine Commander, so that it was impossible to make any mistakes. He even had knowledge of the enemy's next moves (Exodus 9:30, 35).

Because of Pharaoh's continued vacillation, it was necessary for Moses to appear before him many times. As plague followed plague, some of the Egyptians realised that Moses possessed the power to exercise complete control over their environment, and left to themselves would probably have relented, but Pharaoh was less amenable. Yet his policy of standing firm began to look foolish as blow upon blow struck at the very life of the nation. Moses, however, became more confident as time went on and final emancipation drew nearer. God's unfailing faithfulness to His people was obvious to all, inspiring His servant Moses to say to Pharaoh, "We will go with our young and with our old, with our sons and with our daughters, with our flocks and with our herds will we go; for we must hold a feast unto the LORD" (Exodus 10:9), and, "there shall not an hoof be left behind" (Exodus 10:26). When the king threatened Moses with death if he should return to the palace he was equal to the challenge. ""You have spoken well. I will never see your face again," he said, for the last fatal plague was imminent and the Israelites were about to leave Egypt in great haste (Exodus 10:28, 29 NKJV).

In case some should think that Moses made a mistake in saying this, and that Exodus 11:4-8 records another meeting with Pharaoh, it may be said that verses 1 to 3 of this chapter are simply a parenthesis to explain Moses' opening statement and the next five verses record the rest of the interview. The "hot anger" with which Moses left the presence of Pharaoh for the last time showed his disgust at the king's continued obstinacy and his God-given ascendancy over the Egyptians.

That night in complete accord with the word of God through His servant Moses, all the first-born sons of the Egyptians died and Pharaoh's servants implored the Israelites to leave, heaping money and goods on them as they went. So the tyrant king was humbled because he tried to pit his power against God, and his people learnt from bitter experience that retribution falls upon those who oppose God. "He that sitteth in the heavens shall laugh: the Lord shall have them in derision" said the psalmist of those rulers who take counsel together against the Lord, and he adds the good advice, "Now therefore be wise O ye kings: be instructed, ye judges of the earth. Serve the LORD with fear, and rejoice with trembling" (Psalm 2). Present day rulers would do well to listen to the warning of Scripture.

The hardening of Pharaoh's heart has been the subject of much discussion and conjecture. Unbelievers have suggested that since God hardened his heart it was not therefore an act of Pharaoh's own volition and he should not have been held accountable. Yet it should be noted that it was only when the sixth plague came that the Lord hardened the king's heart. Prior to that it is recorded, "His heart was hardened", an action which must have been of his own choosing, for later (Exodus 8:32) it is written, "Pharaoh hardened his heart this time also". The principle is here illustrated that it is not until man has himself barred the way back to God that God rejects him.

But it may be objected that Scripture itself states that God raised up Pharaoh in order to show His power to Egypt and to the world (Romans 9:17) and that this implies that Pharaoh was not personally responsible for the results of his actions. Scripture teaches however that man's freedom of choice and God's sovereignty are two principles which act together in all human decisions. To man they appear contradictory but with God they are perfectly compatible. The human mind cannot fathom this mystery for it is hidden in the unsearchable counsels of the Godhead. The similar false philosophy that crime is the result of a man's upbringing, environment or other external cause, is popular today and glosses over his responsibility to those in authority and to his Maker.

We have briefly commented in this chapter on the short period in Bible history when the paths of two great men crossed: Pharaoh, great in men's eyes, and Moses, great with God. Moses lived a further forty years, and high commendation for his faithfulness is eternally recorded in holy Scripture (Hebrews

3:5). In contrast, Pharaoh disappeared into obscurity, but the plagues and the victory over the elite of the Egyptian army became part of Israel's history, to be recounted as evidence of the power of God and His care for His people (Exodus 18:8-11; Psalm 78:12-54; 106:7-12). Ever since these events took place countless readers of God's word have been impressed by this display of divine power, so fulfilling the scripture to Pharaoh, "But indeed for this purpose I have raised you up, that I may show My power in you, and that My name may be declared in all the earth" (Exodus 9:16; Romans 9:17).

CHAPTER FIVE: THE PASSOVER (JOHN MAWHINNEY)

"**B**y faith he kept the passover, and the sprinkling of the blood, that the destroyer of the firstborn should not touch them". (Hebrews 11:28). And so the Holy Spirit attributes to one man, Moses, what was done by the whole people of Israel. I find this to be most fitting, for Moses was a true leader, shepherd and guide, and he set them an example in carrying out the commands of God, fully meriting the testimony which God gave of him, "He is faithful in all My house" (Numbers 12:7 NKJV).

It seems clear that Moses knew very little of the mighty power of God when he went in to Pharaoh the first time with the command from God, "Let My people go that they may serve Me." For when Pharaoh refused, he came back to God disappointed, and with the reproach on his lips, "Neither have You delivered Your people at all" (Exodus 5:23). But when he went into Pharaoh for the last time, he had experienced the mighty power of God in the nine plagues that had fallen upon the Egyptians, and so he speaks with full assurance to Pharaoh: "And all these your servants shall come down to me and bow down to me, saying, 'Get out, and all the people who follow you!' After that I will go out.". And he went out from Pharaoh in great anger" (Exodus 11:8 NKJV). No doubt he was amazed at the stubbornness and hardness of heart that had been displayed by Pharaoh. He then received instructions from God as to the keeping of the passover, these instructions he passed on to the elders, and they, in turn, passed them on to the people.

We know that the sacrifices and offerings of the Old Testament point forward to the great sacrifice and offering of our Lord Jesus Christ on Calvary, and there can be no doubt that this is so with the passover in Egypt. Paul makes that very clear in 1 Corinthians 5:7 (NKJV), "For our Passover has also been sacrificed, even Christ", and Peter also speaks of being "redeemed ... with precious blood, as of a lamb without blemish and without spot, even the blood of Christ" (1 Peter 1:18, 19).

The lamb taken for the passover had to be without blemish (Exodus 12:5). And so the Holy Spirit brings before us a shadow or type of the sinless perfection of our Lord Jesus Christ. While it was an easy thing to get a lamb without blemish, or any clean beast without one, (at the dedication of the temple, the great peace offering consisted of 22,000 oxen and 120,000 sheep, all without blemish) it was not an easy thing to get a man without blemish. Of all the men who have ever lived on this earth, or will ever live on it, there is only one Man who has lived without sin. The Lord Jesus Christ is the only Man who answered to this condition of the passover lamb, "Your lamb shall be without blemish".

Whatever age the lamb may have been when it was taken from the flock on the tenth day of the first month (one month, two months, three months, or whatever it was), it was to be kept up until the 14th day and then slain, so that it should be obvious to us all that the lamb's life was divided into two parts. For one month, two months, six months or whatever it was, it was with the flock, the rest of the sheep, just one of them, and for four days, the 10th to the 14th, it was set apart, marked off to be the sacrifice, and it was open to all to see that it fulfilled the condition, and was without blemish. And it should be clear to us all that it was the same lamb during both parts of its life, and if it was without blemish here, from the 10th to the 14th day, then it must also have been without blemish during the former part of its life when it was with the rest of the sheep. So also must it be with our Lord Jesus Christ.

We know His life was divided into two parts. He was about 30 years old when He began to teach (Luke 3:23). For the first 30 years of His life He was a private person living in Nazareth, working as a carpenter, no teaching, no miracles, no undue attention drawn to Himself. And for about three and a half years afterwards, He was a public figure, a teacher sent from God, claiming to be the Messiah of Israel, and the very Son of God from heaven, supporting His claims by His mighty works, and claiming to be without sin, "Which of you convicts Me of sin?" (John 8:46 NKJV). If He claimed to be without sin during His public ministry, then He must also have been without sin when He was a private person living in Nazareth. One sin at any time in His life would have made Christ a sinner, and He would not have answered to that fundamental condition relative to the passover lamb, "Your lamb shall be without blemish". The great proof of the sinlessness of Christ lies not in the fact that men could not convict Him of sin, but it lies rather in this most precious truth that He was accepted by God as our passover on Calvary. Any sin in Christ, any blemish in Him, and He would have been rejected as unfit by God, for what was true of Eliab the eldest son of Jesse, is true of all men, and also true of Christ, "Man looks at the outward appearance, but the LORD looks at the heart" (1 Samuel 16:7 NKJV). He who looks at the heart saw the inward purity of His beloved Son, and accepted Him as the fulfilment of the passover lamb in Egypt. Because of this Paul could say, "Our Passover also hath been sacrificed, even Christ". His precious blood provides a safe shelter from the coming wrath of God to all those who put their trust in Him:

By Christ the sinless Lamb of God

The precious blood was shed,

When He fulfilled God's holy word,

And suffered in our stead.

I would like to dwell longer on the precious theme of the sinlessness of Christ, but I must pass on after one more comment upon it. We know the bad reputation Nazareth seems to have had, "Can any good thing come out of Nazareth?" From that place that had the bad name, the sweet savour of a sanctified life ascended to God as the hymn writer has written:

Attaining manhood's ripeness,

Midst sinners sinless He

And though in human likeness,

From human errors free."

At the end of that first period of His life, when He was baptized by John in the Jordan, God gave testimony to the great pleasure He had had in Him, when He said, "This is My beloved Son, in whom I am well pleased" (Matthew 3:17).

The death of the firstborn was the tenth and last plague to fall upon the Egyptians, and it was to save the firstborn of Israel's sons that God gave to Moses the instructions about the passover. There is one vital and important difference between this, the last plague, and all the other plagues and judgements that had fallen upon the Egyptians. From the fourth plague, the plague of flies, God had put a difference between the Israelites and the Egyptians. In the first three plagues the magicians of Egypt had contested against Moses and Aaron, but after their failure to turn dust into lice, they retired from the contest, confessing, "This is the finger of God", and God now says, "I will make a difference between My people and your people" (Exodus 8:23 NKJV). God put this division or difference between the Israelites and the Egyptians in all the remaining plagues, just because they were His people.

When it came to the death of the firstborn in the last of the plagues the difference between the two peoples is maintained. But it rests now on another cause, or has another foundation, and that is the blood of the passover lamb. The difference between the two peoples is not now because. one is the people of God and the other is not, but because there is the blood of the lamb on the lintel and side posts of the doors The firstborn sons of Israel were in danger here as well as the firstborn sons of the Egyptians, and the only thing that could save them was the blood of the lamb on the door posts. If Israel had been exempt from judgement in this plague just because they were the people of God, then that would have meant they would have been redeemed without blood. The very fact that they were in danger from the destroying angel, as well as the Egyptians, brings in the Iamb. The lamb is a shadow of Christ, and in this is the voice of God to all men today.

If Israel could have been redeemed without blood in that far off day that would mean that men today could be saved or redeemed without Christ, and such a thing is an utter impossibility. We may as well try to live without breathing as seek to get saved apart from Christ, "Apart from shedding of blood there is no remission" (Hebrews 9:22). God's word in that day is His word for today also, "When I see the blood, I will pass over you."

"How calm the judgment hour will pass

To all who do obey

The word of God, and trust the blood,

And make that word their stay."

The people of Israel were to remember the passover ever afterwards in all their generations, and they were to celebrate it yearly, in the first month, on the 14th day of the month. Certain instructions were given to them as to how they were to celebrate it. It is not possible to enter into those instructions in any detail in this chapter, but I would pass this comment. To the generation that came out of Egypt, especially the firstborn sons, the yearly celebration of the passover would indeed be a very solemn occasion, and a cause of great rejoicing. They were the ones who really passed through it, but as that generation passed away, and other generations succeeded, then the memory of the passover would lose much of its force, and succeeding generations celebrated a passover, a deliverance, that belonged to their forefathers. It was not theirs personally.

There lies the great difference between their remembrance of their passover, and the remembrance of "our Passover, even Christ". At the weekly remembrance of our Lord Jesus Christ, when God's people come together to remember Him in the breaking of the bread, we meet to remember a Redeemer, a Deliverer, a Saviour, who is our very own; we each remember a personal Saviour. If He is also the Saviour of our fathers, we rejoice in that, but the great and precious truth is this, we meet to remember One who is indeed, "OUR PASSOVER".

Perhaps the people of Israel afterwards never gave a thought to the lamb that died that night in Egypt, but we must remember Christ, not only in this special way in the breaking of the bread, but every day of our lives, He had to pass through more, much more than any lamb in Egypt. Who amongst us yet has fully grasped what the Lord meant that night when He said, "With desire I have desired to eat this passover with you before I suffer" (Luke 22:15)?

Just one word more - the lamb died in Egypt, and that was the end of it, but our Passover has been raised from the dead, and sits now at the right hand of God. Blessed be His name!

"And we have known redemption, Lord,

From bondage worse than theirs by far,

Sin held us by a stronger cord,

But by Thy mercy free we are.

CHAPTER SIX: THE RED SEA AND THE WILDERNESS (JOHN DRAIN)

———

T he joy with which the children of Israel must have left Egypt and its tyranny was soon lost. Dismay and murmuring took its place. The Lord had commanded the departing Israelites to take a particular route, and His declared purpose was to bring about a situation in which He would get honour upon Pharaoh and his host, and would also establish in the minds of the Egyptians that the God of the Hebrews was indeed the LORD, the living and true God. The outworking of this purpose brought an early test to the leadership of Moses.

As the children of Israel began to take stock of their position they saw themselves faced and flanked by physical obstacles. Behind them closed in the army of Egypt. They were trapped. Panic began to grip the people. Cutting sneers were hurled at Moses, but that noble man rose supremely above the crisis. His faith was in God and in the triumph of His purpose. "Fear ye not", he said, "Stand still, and see the salvation of the LORD, which He will work for you today ... the LORD shall fight for you, and ye shall hold your peace" (Exodus 14:13,14). Moses saw the Lord rather than the difficulties, the Lord who had promised and who was able to perform; hence the good words which stilled the people.

It often happens that in the experiences of life we become obsessed with the problems which confront us. We look everywhere but to God. Our great Leader says to us, "Let not your heart be troubled: ye believe in God, believe also in Me ... These things have I spoken unto you, that in Me ye may have peace. In the world ye have tribulation: but be of good cheer; I have overcome the world" (John 14:1; 16:33).

God's way for His people was a forward way. It was neither deviation nor retreat: "Thy way was in the sea" (Psalm 77:19). By divine command Moses lifted up his rod, the symbol of authority and power, and stretched his hand over the sea. There followed an amazing miracle. The Lord "caused His glorious Arm to go at the right hand of Moses". He "dried up the sea" and "made the depths of the sea a way for the redeemed to pass over" (see Isaiah 63:12 and 51:10). Into this way poured the many thousands of the redeemed Israelites. They went down into the place of death, and, in resurrection-like experience, they rose triumphantly on the wilderness side of the sea. From this vantage ground they surveyed the manifestation of God's authority and power, His goodness and His severity, His salvation and His judgement. The effect was salutary: "Israel saw the great work which the LORD did upon the Egyptians, and the people feared the LORD: and they believed in the LORD, and in His servant Moses" (Exodus 14:31). The leadership of Moses was confirmed. His authority was established. The historical record of the happenings at the Red Sea would undoubtedly have encouraged in readers a profound appreciation of the power of God. But something of the spiritual significance of what happened would have been missed but for the inspired statement in 1 Corinthians 10:1,2, "Our fathers were all under the cloud, and all passed through the sea; and were all baptized unto Moses in the cloud and in the sea".

The cloud was a visible token of the presence of God, particularly for the purpose of leading and protecting. Moses was the appointed leader of the people. In the purpose of the Lord the children of Israel had died to Egypt and to its king. They were buried and raised again to be under new authority and to enter into the possibilities of a new life and the privileges of new service. God's chosen leader Moses was to be acknowledged as their leader.

New Testament scriptures indicate very clearly that the great Leader of God's people today is the Lord Jesus Christ, in whom full divine authority has been vested. In the baptism of disciples in water there is an acknowledgement of this authority and a pictorial demonstration that believers in Christ have died with Him, are buried and raised to walk in newness of life. They have been baptized unto Christ, from then on to live in subjection and obedience to Him.

With a newborn joy of deliverance in their hearts the children of Israel, now separated from Egypt by the rolling waters of the Red Sea, burst forth in singing. An inspired song was on their lips. The leader of the praise was Moses. It must have been an amazing experience when the song of the redeemed rent the air in that desert setting. But that song went far beyond the vault of the skies. It reached the throne of heaven. It reached the heart of God. Great indeed must have been His joy as He looked upon that vast assemblage of men and women whom He loved and whom He had redeemed from bondage, and as He heard the song of praise. And there, leading the praise of the congregation, was Moses, the man of God.

This song of victory will yet again be heard, sung, perhaps, with greater fervour born out of deeper appreciation. We refer to the time yet future when there will be heard the singing of them that come victorious from the bondage and oppression of the beast. "They sing the song of Moses the servant of God, and the song of the Lamb, saying, Great and marvellous are Thy works, O Lord God, the Almighty; righteous and true are Thy ways, Thou King of the ages" (Revelation 15:3). What a day that will be for the Lamb! And what a day it will be for Moses!

In the epistle to the Hebrews, we have an illuminating exposition of the privileges of service extended to those in the present dispensation who, in response to the conditional side of the New Covenant, are gathered to be God's people, God's house. One very profound revelation in this exposition is found in the words, "In the midst of the congregation will I sing Thy praise" (Hebrews 2:12). There can be no doubt that this quotation from Psalm 22 applies specifically to Christ. The conception is entrancing. God the Son is the great Leader in the song of praise raised to God by His people. The realization of this is delightful. But it bows our hearts in holy, solemn awe.

Israel's song was short-lived. In a few days' time a spirit of murmuring, like a heath fire, swept through the people. In the wilderness there was no water supply. One possible source seemed useless because its waters were bitter. Very quickly the people's reliance in the Lord crumbled. Again the brunt of the murmuring fell on Moses. What could he do? Once more we see the wisdom and strength of this leader. He cried unto the Lord. The Lord heard. The Lord answered. What a lesson for times of difficulty!

Refreshed by the springs and palm trees of Elim the Israelites, halfway through the second month after their departure from Egypt, set forward on their march. A fresh crisis arose. There was no food. Again faith in God perished. Again the plague of murmuring smote the people. Again Moses was the special target. "You have brought us out into this wilderness to kill this whole assembly with hunger" (Exodus 16:3). The man's patience must have been sorely tried. Would he give up? Was the task worth the trouble? Was there not a legitimate limit to what he should take in abuse and insult? But Moses was a meek man. And he lived close to the Lord. Once again God intervened to meet the need by miraculous provision.

Shortly after this experience the people reached Rephidim. A new test came to prove them. There was no water. The recollection of previous gracious and powerful provision by their God did not influence the people. The floodgates of murmuring were again opened. Moses had to endure another spate of abuse and threat. As he cried to the Lord he said, "They be almost ready to stone me" (Exodus 17:4). In meeting the need of the people on this occasion the Lord committed to His servant Moses one of the most solemn and significant tasks of that godly man's activities. The Lord said, "Behold, I will stand before thee there upon the rock in Horeb; and thou shalt smite the rock, and there shall come water of out it, that the people may drink". The One who gave the bread from heaven gave also the water from the rock. The provision was miraculous and supernatural. The Lord stood upon the rock. Moses smote with his rod. The water gushed out. The people drank of a spiritual rock, "and the rock was Christ". It is through Christ, the smitten One of Golgotha, that all the blessings of divine favour have reached mankind.

Murmuring is a pernicious scourge. Where it exists there is destruction. It will destroy an individual. It will destroy a nation. It breeds a discontent which will soon lead to lawlessness and rebellion. And it opens doors for hostile forces to attack. As we reflect on the murmuring which characterized the attitude of the Israel people during the first few weeks after their leaving Egypt we feel the force of the words, "Then came Amalek, and fought with Israel in Rephidim" (Exodus 17:8).

The attack of Amalek presented to Moses a situation of fresh difficulty. War had come. This was a new experience. Moses, who looked to the Lord for bread and meat and water, now looked to the Lord for victory. Two important activities emerged from Moses' disposition of his resources. To a young man, Joshua, would be given the responsibility of leading the fighting men against the attackers. Moses himself, with Aaron and Hur, would climb the hill to hold aloft the rod of God. There was a definite relationship between the sword in the hand of Joshua and the rod in the hand of Moses. Moses raised his hand to the throne of God calling down authority and power for the hand of Joshua which was raised against Amalek. The task which Moses assumed was most arduous. But there were others to help him. He had partners. The battle swayed backwards and forwards. It was tense. But the Lord gave victory.

We are grateful for One on the throne of heaven who, without intermission, without fatigue, pleads our cause. We are grateful too for One who is in us to fight the enemy. Human resources are valueless. On the other hand we have our responsibilities. In the power of the Spirit the enemy must be opposed. But let us all, those who lead and those who are led, take the point. Victory in conflict comes from victory in prayer.

In Exodus 18 we read the moving story of the arrival of Jethro, the father-in-law of Moses, in the camp of Israel. Moses might have seized this opportunity to pour out a tale of woe as to what he had suffered from the people. But no, he was above that. His sincere and glowing testimony to what the Lord had done for Israel led the man Jethro to say with great joy, "Now I know that the LORD is greater than all gods" (Exodus 18:11). It is distressing to think that the public witness of the people of God can be besmirched and weakened by unnecessary exposures of the failures which, sad to say, beset us. What God in grace and power has done should more frequently be our theme. It will be more convincing and attractive.

When Jethro learned that Moses had undertaken the mammoth task of hearing alone the causes of all the people, and of delivering judgement and teaching he offered sound advice. But he qualified its acceptance by Moses with the words, "If ... God command thee so". The counsel submitted proposed the devolution and distribution of authority and responsibility. Thus the basis of judicial administration and rule was broadened. Great men have big hearts, but there are human limitations which must be recognized. Moses learned this. It is good for the people of God when there are men fitted and ready to share the burdens of rule, and to do so in the spirit of true subjection to one another, in a common subjection to the Lord.

CHAPTER SEVEN: MEDIATOR OF THE COVENANT (R. LINDSAY)

———

A high point of Israel's national history came at Horeb, in the third month after their deliverance from Egypt. Having come to the wilderness of Sinai, they camped before the mount. The scene was awe-inspiring. "Mount Sinai was altogether on smoke, because the LORD descended upon it in fire: and the smoke thereof ascended as the smoke of a furnace, and the whole mount quaked greatly ... the voice of the trumpet waxed louder and louder" (Exodus 19:18,19). The people had been warned not to touch the mount, on penalty of death. And as they saw such evidences of the presence of Jehovah, "all the people that were in the camp trembled" (Exodus 19:16). At the command of the Lord, Moses went up to the top of the mount. As he reminded Israel towards the end of his life, "I stood between the LORD and you at that time, to shew you the word of the LORD. For ye were afraid because of the fire" (Deuteronomy 5:5).

On the mountain, Moses listened to the voice of Jehovah as He instructed him to remind Israel of what He had already done for them in redeeming them from Egypt. Now a new vista was being opened before them, as the Lord held out the promise, "You shall be a special treasure to Me above all people; for all the earth is Mine. And you shall be to Me a kingdom of priests and a holy nation" (Exodus 19:5,6 NKJV). The bondmen of

Egypt - now to be the people of God! But the promise was conditional upon their obedience. The word was, "If you will indeed obey My voice, and keep My covenant, then you shall be ..." The people's response was unanimous: "All that the LORD hath spoken will we do and be obedient", they answered, and on this basis the Lord proceeded to give Moses the commandments, judgements and statutes by which Israel, as His people, would henceforth be governed. The moment at which the covenant was entered into was an exceedingly solemn one:

"Today you have proclaimed the Lord to be your God, and that you will walk in His ways and keep His statutes, His commandments, and His judgments, and that you will obey His voice. 18 Also today the Lord has proclaimed you to be His special people, just as He promised you, that you should keep all His commandments, 19 and that He will set you high above all nations which He has made, in praise, in name, and in honor, and that you may be a holy people to the Lord your God, just as He has spoken" (Deuteronomy 26:17-19 NKJV).

THE TERMS OF THE COVENANT

The terms of the covenant given by God through Moses are detailed in Exodus 20:1-23:19. It legislated for every aspect of Israel's life. The law came under three headings:

(1) The Commandments (Exodus 20). The first four commandments deal with the people's responsibilities towards God, and hinge around their love for Him; the remaining six refer to their

duties towards each other. The order is surely clear and instructive. No person or thing must be allowed to usurp the place which alone belongs to God. He must ever occupy the first place in the lives and affections of His people. The Lord Jesus reinforced this principle in Matthew 22:37-40, where He said that the first and great commandment is to "love the Lord thy God with all thy heart, and with all thy soul, and with all thy mind". The second, He said, is like unto it, "Thou shalt love thy neighbour as thyself".

(2) The Judgements (Exodus 21:1-23:9) governed the social and commercial life of the nation. Relationships between masters and servants, injuries to individuals, and damage to or loss of possessions are among the matters covered.

(3) The Statutes (Exodus 23:10-19) decreed that the Sabbath rests should be observed, and set out Israel's obligations in connection with the Feasts of Jehovah.

The law was, indeed, comprehensive. It was given by God in order that His people might be governed by it, and He required that it should be obeyed implicitly. Failure to do so would be visited by retribution from the angel who was to go before them on their journey (Exodus 23:21).

Just as Israel through Moses received the statutes and judgements, so also the Lord has legislated for the lives of His

New Covenant people. The teaching of the Lord Jesus and His apostles determines the standards by which our lives must be governed. "The Faith ... once for all delivered unto the saints", Jude called it. To this we must give unhesitating obedience. We must stand fast in the Faith (1 Corinthians 16:13) and contend earnestly for it (Jude 3).

THE BLOOD OF SPRINKLING

When the words of the law were spoken to and accepted by the people, oxen were slain for burnt offerings and peace offerings, and the altar and the people were sprinkled with the blood of the covenant. Clearly, this presents a different aspect of truth from the blood of the passover sacrifice, which was shed in Egypt. That was the blood of their redemption; this, the blood of sanctification which placed upon them the obligation of obedience. The New Testament answer to this can be seen in 1 Peter 1:1,2, where the sojourners of the dispersion are described as being "elect ... according to the foreknowledge of God the Father, in sanctification of the Spirit, unto obedience and sprinkling of the blood of Jesus Christ". A similar thought is expressed in Hebrews 12: 22-24, "Ye are come ... to Jesus the Mediator of a new covenant, and to the blood of sprinkling that speaketh better than that of Abel. See that ye refuse not Him that speaketh". God's New Covenant people are responsible, as were Israel under the Old Covenant, to render obedience to the commandments of the Lord.

It was on the ground of their obedience that the Lord constituted Israel "a peculiar treasure, a kingdom of priests and an holy nation. Likewise, it was a people who had purified their souls in obedience to the truth whom Peter described as "an elect race, a royal priesthood, a holy nation, a people for God's own possession" (1 Peter 2:9). The similarity in the language is striking, and we cannot escape the great privilege, albeit one which carries a heavy responsibility of obedience. Hebrews 10: 26-31 describes in solemn language the severity of the judgement of God on him who "hath trodden under foot the Son of God, and hath counted the blood of the covenant, wherewith he was sanctified, an unholy thing". May the people of God today guard themselves from the dangers of disobedience.

THE COVENANT AND THE HOUSE

Associated with the Covenant were the feasts of Jehovah to which all the males of Israel were to come three times in the year. The instructions were explicit: they were to "appear before the LORD thy God in the place which He shall choose" (Deuteronomy 16:16). There, in the place of the Name, were found the altar and the mercy seat, and it was to this place that the godly Israelite ever turned. "Now even the first covenant had ordinances of divine service, and its sanctuary, a sanctuary of this world. For there was a tabernacle prepared, the first ..." (Hebrews 9:1,2). And in the house of God, whether the tabernacle in the wilderness, the temple built by Solomon or the house rebuilt by the remnant returned from Babylon, Israel fulfilled her function as a kingdom of priests. But the house was an earthly house, and its sanctuary but a copy of the heavenly sanctuary. "The way into the holy place hath not yet been made manifest, while as the first tabernacle is yet standing" (Hebrews 9:8).

By contrast, under the New Covenant the house is a spiritual one, and the sanctuary is heavenly. Through our Great High Priest, who ministers there, the people of God enter into this heavenly sanctuary, as a holy priesthood, to offer up spiritual sacrifices (1 Peter 2.5). The clear teaching of Hebrews chapters 9 and 10 is that, whereas under the Mosaic covenant the high priest alone could enter the sanctuary, and that but once in the year, Christ has entered in once for all through His own blood, now to appear as Great High Priest before the face of God for us. Through Him, the holy priesthood now draws near, and in the heavenly sanctuary we present our sacrifice of praises, even the fruit of lips which make confession to His Name (Hebrews 13:15): "Having therefore, brethren, boldness to enter into the holy place by the blood of Jesus, by the way which He dedicated for us ... through the veil, that is to say, His flesh; and having a great Priest over the house of God; let us draw near ... " (Hebrews 10:19-22).

THE MEDIATOR

The scene at Sinai was an awe-inspiring one. The demonstration of divine glory in the flashing lightning, the reverberating thunder and the voice of the trumpet had caused the fear of the Lord so to grip the hearts of Israel that they said to Moses, "You speak with us, and we will hear; but let not God speak with us, lest we die" (Exodus 20:19 NKJV). Thus Moses, at the wish of the people and the command of the Lord, drew near into the thick darkness where God was. There, on Israel's behalf, he stood before the Lord, and heard from His mouth the words of the law which he relayed to Israel. As the one who stood between God and the people, Moses became the mediator, at whose hand the law was given, and thus a type of the Lord Jesus Christ, "the Mediator of a better Covenant, which hath been enacted upon better promises (Hebrews 8:6).

The Lord Jesus, however, stands related to the New Covenant, not only as its Mediator, but as its Surety (Hebrews 7:22), and its Sacrifice. The New Covenant, under which we serve God today, has been sealed by His own precious blood (Hebrews 12:24). Well may we contemplate solemnly His words to the disciples in the upper room, "This cup is the new covenant in My blood, even that which is poured out for you" (Luke 22:20).

THE NEW COVENANT

The covenant given through Moses has been superseded. The death of the Lord Jesus has opened the way for a new covenant, made with another people. Israel's disobedience to the will of God led to their rejection as His people, and they have been set aside, for the time being, "They continued not in My covenant, and I regarded them not, saith the Lord" (Hebrews 8:9). A day is ahead, however, in which the Lord will once again put His laws into their mind, and write them on their heart. He will make another covenant with the house of Israel and with the house of Judah (Hebrews 8:8), and the nation will be re-established as the people of God.

But, for the present, God has taken up a people with whom He has established a new covenant. They occupy a position of high privilege - a spiritual house, a holy nation, a people for God's own possession (1 Peter 2). Their responsibility to be obedient to the Faith is vital to their continuance in this spiritual heritage, lest their place as God's people should be forfeited, as was Israel's: "Wherefore, receiving a kingdom that cannot be shaken, let us have grace, whereby we may offer service well-pleasing to God with reverence and awe: for our God is a consuming fire" (Hebrews 12: 28,29).

CHAPTER EIGHT: FAITHFUL IN ALL GOD'S HOUSE (ALAN TOMS)

B y comparison and contrast, the writer to the Hebrews presents the surpassing excellence of the Person of Christ. "Better than" is one of the key phrases that run through the epistle, and in chapter 3 Christ is shown to be better than Moses by so much as the one who builds a house, in whose mind the design is conceived and through whose skill the building reaches completion, has more honour than the house itself. That is true of any building, of course, but in this paragraph it is the building of God's house which is under consideration. In this house Moses was a servant. But now Christ is Son over God's house.

We get a glimpse of the great truth of God dwelling among men in Genesis 28 when He brought Jacob to Bethel, but not until He had redeemed Jacob's posterity out of the bondage of Egypt, baptized them in the waters of the Red Sea and heard their pledge of obedience to all that He commanded, did God expressly say "Let them make Me a sanctuary; that I may dwell among them". To Moses was entrusted the responsibility of receiving from God the pattern of this house and of supervising its building in absolute conformity to it. He was God's servant (Greek: therapon, minister) in this tremendous assignment, and the divine approbation is recorded for all time, "Moses indeed was faithful in all God's house (R.V. margin) as a servant". He filled the role of both apostle, sent by God to His people, and prophet, in whose mouth God put His words (Deuteronomy 18:18), and faithfully Moses conveyed to the people every word which God had spoken.

THE PATTERN GIVEN

The house which was to be built was, as we have seen, to be according to a divine pattern. The Lord called Moses to the mountain of God where he was shown the heavenly pattern and then sent down to build in the wilderness a dwelling-place for God which answered to it. Careful reflection will impress upon us the immensity of the task with which he was entrusted.

One of my boyhood memories is of being invited to the home of one of the elders of the church of God in which my early years were spent. He was a gentleman greatly loved and respected by all who knew him. The wonders of God's creation were but one of the studies with which he had furnished his mind, and I remember him showing us under his microscope the finest and most delicate surgical needle he had been able to procure, and alongside it was the sting of 'a bee. The contrast was striking, not only in the much greater thickness of the needle in relation to the bee sting, but even more so in that the needle under magnification was seen to be rough and pitted whereas the sting of the bee was smooth and flawless. We learned in a forcible way that down to the tiniest details of His vast creation God's work is perfect.

Bearing that point in mind we reflect upon what Moses must have seen as God showed him the heavenly sanctuary, the true tabernacle which the Lord pitched, not man (Hebrews 8:2). Here was the throne of God, where the innumerable hosts of angels worship Him day and night. "Honour and majesty are before Him: strength and beauty are in His sanctuary" (Psalm 96:6). What a glorious sight Moses was privileged to see! And every detail of it was impressed upon the mind of this faithful servant. He had been instructed in all the wisdom of Egypt, until he was mighty in his words and works. This training may well have helped him to retain much of what he saw, but doubtless it would require the working of the Spirit of God upon his mind to bring to his remembrance the infinite detail of the design of the whole and of its many parts. Certainly we can be sure that God who is so precise in all His ways would not allow the smallest detail to be overlooked. And having had it thus implanted upon his mind, Moses then conveyed to the people all that God had shown him. Four times over these or similar words occur: "... see to it that you make *them* according to the pattern which was shown you on the mountain" (Exodus 25:40 NKJV).

THE WORK PROSECUTED

Exceedingly busy months would follow for Moses. It is true he did not do the work himself. Bezalel and Oholiab were raised up by God, filled with the Spirit of God in wisdom and in understanding and in knowledge and in all manner of workmanship. And not only were they gifted to do the work themselves, but also to teach others, so that many wise-hearted men joined in the task, and there were the women also who spun the goats' hair in their tents. But to one man alone had been given the pattern. He had seen the heavenly thing which these men, themselves guided by the Spirit of God, were now copying on earth. Surely we are not wandering into the realm of imagination when we suggest that constantly these workmen would refer to Moses for instruction and guidance during the nine months, or less, that the work was in progress. Moses would be at pains to ensure that every detail was according to the pattern which God had so carefully shown him, and which the Spirit of God would now so precisely bring back to his remembrance.

At last the long task was completed and on the first day of the first month of the second year the tabernacle of the tent of meeting was reared up. With a sense of admiration we read, "Thus did Moses: according to all that the LORD commanded him, so did he" (Exodus 40:16). "So Moses finished the work" (verse 33) and God showed His complete approval of all that had been done when the cloud covered the tent of meeting and the glory of the Lord filled the tabernacle. What a testimony to the faithfulness of God's servant. No wonder God's anger was later kindled against Miriam and Aaron when they spoke against Moses in Numbers 12. "My servant Moses ... He is faithful in all My house. I speak with him face to face, even plainly, and not in dark sayings; and he sees the form of the Lord. Why then were you not afraid to speak against My servant Moses?" (verses 7,8 NKJV).

THE PATTERN UNDER THE NEW COVENANT

In the present dispensation there is in the purpose of God a spiritual house which is the counterpart of the material house which was built by Moses. The building of this house began on the day of Pentecost. Later God called a man who, like Moses, was to be a faithful servant in the building of His spiritual house. The dual gifts of apostle and prophet were combined in this servant also, who described himself as a minister of Christ and a steward of the mysteries of God (1 Corinthians 4:1). Like Moses too, Paul spent some time in Arabia alone with God. How long he was there we do not know but three years elapsed from the time of his conversion to his going up to Jerusalem and presenting himself to his fellow-apostles, and those three years were spent between Arabia and Damascus. The pattern of teaching which was given to him was as precious to Paul as the pattern given to Moses had been to that faithful servant.

In regard to the gospel which he preached, he wrote "Neither did I receive it from man, nor was I taught it, but it came to me through revelation of Jesus Christ" (Galatians 1:12). And that which was thus revealed he faithfully delivered to others. "I delivered unto you first of all that which also I received" (1 Corinthians 15:3). He received it, preached it, delivered it, and often contended for it, for when false brethren tried to introduce another gospel, he "gave place in the way of subjection, no, not for an hour; that the truth of the gospel might continue with you" (Galatians 2:5).

And so it was with every facet of divine truth. "I received of the Lord that which also I delivered unto you" he wrote in connection with the Lord's supper. As he received it, so he delivered it. Nothing would persuade him to add to it, or take from it, even in the smallest detail, and when as was often the case, it was unacceptable to those to whom he preached, still he shrank not from declaring the whole counsel of God. It was his stewardship, and "it is required in stewards that a man be found faithful". He was faithful unto death, and when his strenuous labours we're almost over he wrote to Timothy, his child in the faith, "Hold the pattern of sound words which thou hast heard from me, in faith and love which is in Christ Jesus" (2 Timothy 1:13).

TEACHING OTHERS

Another faithful man was ready to carry on the work, but if there was to be continuity he must pass on to others what he had learned. So among the last words which Paul wrote we find this important instruction, "the things which thou hast heard from me among many witnesses, the same commit thou to faithful men, who shall be able to teach others also" (2 Timothy 2:2). Four generations of men are envisaged in this verse. From Paul to Timothy, from Timothy to faithful men, and from those faithful men to others. Only thus would the line of succession be assured. It takes faithful men to hold divine truth and never more so than today. "The time will come" warned the apostle, "when they will not endure the sound doctrine; but, having itching ears, will heap to themselves teachers after their own lusts: and will turn away their ears from the truth". It happened long before the apostolic era ended. And it is happening all around us today.

But the pattern given to and faithfully delivered by the apostles and prophets still holds good today. Let those who love their

Bibles never forget that. If God's great desire to dwell amongst men on earth is to continue to be realized then faithful men and women must continue to build to the pattern. And let us never forget also that the God whom we serve is a God of perfection in every detail. Every part of His revealed truth is important. We dare not ignore the smallest detail it we desire to please Him. "Teaching them to observe all things whatsoever I commanded you" was the resurrected Master's parting word to His apostles. We live in days when truth is being assailed on every hand. Even great bulwarks of the Faith are being challenged by men who once stood boldly for them. Never was there a day when faithful men were more needed.

Who will present themselves alive unto God, to learn the pattern of sound words, be assured of it in their own hearts, hold it fast, build to it, contend for it when occasion demands and then pass it on to others? Those who do so will find themselves walking the straightened way, in company with the few, but let us remember it leads to life, and will it not be ample compensation if having served the counsel of God we might hear the divine commendation, "Well done, good and faithful servant ... enter thou into the joy of thy Lord".

CHAPTER NINE: THE PLEADER (JACK FERGUSON)

———

T he law courts of the nations have heard impassioned appeals by brilliant pleaders. Juries have been swayed. Judges may have been affected. These men had power with the human mind.

In Bible history too there have been pleaders. But these men, to use Hosea's expression, "had power with God ... and prevailed". This was pleading at its highest level; profound pleading with God on behalf of Israel (as in the case of Moses, our present study), or the opposite, against them (as in the case of Elijah). These were the supplications of righteous men, which, James tells us, availed much in their working. They were the effectual pleadings of fervent prayer.

These men knew their God. Their intercessions were keenly intelligent in their understanding of the divine will, daring in their demand, brilliant in their presentation. Clearly God loved to be appealed to by such men. And women too. Take for an example of intelligent intercession Hannah's prayer for the needs of God in His holy temple. "O LORD of hosts ... give unto Thine handmaid a man child" (1 Samuel 1:11). "LORD of hosts" - never before in Scripture had this Name reached His ear. It was a woman, reminding Him that He had hosts and she only wanted one. God loved such intelligence in intercession.

Only some three months had passed since Israel was led out in joy from Egypt, and already they were returning in heart to it. They had pledged themselves to the covenant of obedience and for the fifth time Moses climbed Sinai. He went as Israel's mediator, to receive on their behalf the living oracles, the ordinance of angels; little did he realize the dual form his mediation would take.

But God knew, for "known unto God are all His works from the beginning of the world" (Acts 15:18 KJV). If we could foresee the issue of certain courses of action we would never embark on them. We would shrink from failure. But not so the omniscient God. "From the beginning of the world" He has known that enemies will assail His plans and friends will fail in their assignments. Yet nothing deflects Him from His purposes, nor affects His zeal in offering opportunities to men to serve Him. Were it not so He would never initiate any project for the benefit of humankind.

And so it was in the matter of the golden calf. God took Israel at their word in Exodus 24 though He knew they would worship the calf in a matter of days. He gave Moses the pattern of the Tabernacle with the details of the priestly garments and service, knowing that even while He was speaking, Aaron was leading the nation into idolatry. But His knowledge of failure was not allowed to affect the sweetness of the forty days' communion with Moses.

The conduct of the nation at the foot of the mountain was incomprehensible. They had seen the signs in Egypt, the miracle of the Red Sea; they had heard the voice of the living

God from the fires of Sinai. All we can say is, "let him that thinketh he standeth take heed lest he fall". They insisted on the tangible. From the first day Moses knew them they were a people void of faith. Right at the outset they failed in the test of his absence. Their hearts went back to Egypt and its gods. So Aaron took their gold, made a calf for them to worship, and incongruously linked the service with a feast to the Lord. Round the idol they danced in an orgy of loose permissiveness, to what Dr. Strong describes in his concordance as "the scornful whispering (of hostile spectators)".

When their communion was over, God told Moses to leave His presence, for the people whom he (Moses) had brought from Egypt had turned aside to corrupted ways. God just wished to be alone so that His anger might wax hot. Moses was still unaware of the details of the corruption. All he knew was that the fate of the nation was already in the balance with God. To borrow the famous words of Jonathan Edwards in another context, Israel had fallen "into the hands of an angry God". He wished to destroy them completely and to start afresh with Moses.

Through him He would maintain unbroken the covenant of Abraham of the seed and the land, just as through Noah he had maintained the promise of the woman's Seed. But centuries later they sang in Israel that on that day "Moses His chosen stood before Him in the breach, to turn away His wrath, lest He should destroy them" (Psalm 106:23). Later in Israel's history God said, "And I sought for a man among them, that should make up the fence, and stand in the gap before Me for the land, that I should not destroy it: but I found none"

(Ezekiel 22:30). But in the day of the golden calf, Moses the pleader was there to stand in the breach.

His intercession was brief, intelligent, demanding. It was the perfect plea which could not go unanswered. It had three points. The first was that Israel was the Lord's own espoused people, redeemed by such great power. The second was how Egypt would mock the glory of God were He to destroy the people He had just delivered. The third was a nostalgic remembrance of covenant promises to the patriarchs. Again there was as it were a hand "lifted up upon the throne of Jah" (Exodus 17:16 Hebrew margin), and the judgement was stayed.

Then Moses came down and saw for himself the reason for the divine wrath and his own anger waxed hot in turn. He burned the golden calf in the fire (the secret of which remarkable process he may have learned in Egypt) and ground it to fine powder. He scattered the dust in the waters of the brook which descended from the mountain and made Israel drink the bitter water of their sin. Then the old man toiled broken-hearted up the mountain for the sixth time, deeply conscious now of the cause of the divine anger, and the great pleader made his impassioned plea for forgiveness, offering himself in atonement if that were the only way. He was willing to be blotted out of the book of God for Israel's sake, a foreshadowing of the pleading of the nation's other kinsman in Romans 9:3.

Pleaders with God! Abraham interceding for the righteous in Sodom (Genesis 18); Moses for Israel and his own brother in particular (Deuteronomy 9:19,20); Samuel for lamenting

Israel (1 Samuel 7); Amos in the face of devouring locusts and fire (Amos 7:1-6). The memory of the power these men had with God remained in the divine mind, so that centuries later the Lord said to Jeremiah, "Though Moses and Samuel stood before Me, yet My mind could not be toward this people: cast them out of My sight" (Jeremiah 15:1).

Again the centuries passed and a lonely Man cried out in the sorrows of the Tree, "Father, forgive them; for they know not what they do". Then the darkness came down and the Pleader went into abandonment from God for the sin of the world, faintly prefigured in the desolate, sin-bearing scapegoat left alone to die in the wilderness. Then the resurrection morning saw Him ascend where He was before, and the Mediator from Calvary became the Advocate in heaven for all God's children, the High Priest for all His people, in a ministry of intercession which prevails against the charges of the accuser of the brethren.

And so we sing:

Before the throne of God above

I have a strong, a perfect plea

A great High Priest, whose name is Love

Who ever lives and pleads for me.

God still searches among His people for pleaders, and the ministry of intercession; for brothers and sisters who, publicly and privately, will still fill "the golden bowls full of incense". He said to Israel, "I have set watchmen upon thy walls, O

Jerusalem; they shall never hold their peace day nor night: ye that are the LORD's remembrancers, take ye no rest, and give Him no rest (Isaiah 62:6,7). Maybe someone reading this will say, from the heart fervently, "Lord, make me a watchman upon Thy walls, a pleader who will stand in the breach".

CHAPTER TEN: WILDERNESS WANDERINGS (LAURIE BURROWS)

―――――

Israel's journey to the promised land should have been happy and triumphant. The people had at last escaped from the lash of the taskmaster's whip and the long oppression of a foreign despot; with all their needs divinely supplied they were on their way to a land flowing with milk and honey. But such is the perversity of the human heart that most of the story of those years became one of unbelief and rebellion, summed up in the divine comment, "Forty years long was I grieved with that generation" (Psalm 95:10).

The voice of the grumblers was heard even before the Red Sea had been crossed and later there was trouble at the wilderness of Sin when there appeared to be no food to eat, but the Lord "rained bread from heaven" and quails covered the camp (Exodus 14:10-14; 16:1-18). Soon they came to Rephidim where there was no water and they threatened their leader with death, but at the command of the Lord Moses struck the rock in Horeb and water gushed out. After receiving the Law at Sinai, no sooner had they resumed their journey than grumbling broke out once more and some were judged by fire from heaven. Again they hankered after flesh to eat and the Lord satisfied their desire, but a plague broke out among them because of their sin. Then even Aaron and Miriam began to find fault with Moses, but that sin was quickly dealt with also (Numbers 11 and 12).

These sorry events happened during the first two years of the journey, when God was leading His people by planned stages, first to Mount Sinai to receive the Law, then to the wilderness of Paran to establish a base from which entry to the promised land should have been made in a few short weeks. There could have been a triumphant march with all opposition melting away, but instead open mutiny broke out when reports came back from some of the spies that there were giants in the land and cities "fenced up to heaven". The people refused to listen to the sound advice of Joshua and Caleb to put their trust in the Lord, so to all the men of war God said, "Your carcasses shall fall in this wilderness. And your children shall be wanderers ... forty years" (Numbers 14:32-33). Only Joshua and Caleb escaped this judgement. In later years when Moses was reminding the succeeding generation of their responsibilities, he recalled: "The LORD's anger was kindled against Israel, and He made them wander to and fro in the wilderness forty years, until all the generation, that had done evil in the sight of the LORD, was consumed" (Numbers 32:13).

It would appear from a comparison of Numbers 13:26 with Numbers 20:1 and the events which followed that the recorded journeys of the children of Israel fall into two periods: the first takes the record up to the mutiny at Kadesh-barnea described above, and the second deals with the journey from the same place to Canaan thirty-eight years later. Apart from the sin of Korah, Scripture draws a veil over the long interval between, when without obvious divine guidance, they lived aimless lives

until all the men of war who came out of Egypt were dead. It is
to those sterile years that the term "wandering" in this chapter's
title properly applies. It was not until the evil influence of the
rebels had been removed by death that the Lord could again
take up His people and lead them into their inheritance.

The peninsula of Sinai, where they wandered, is inhospitable
in the extreme and is notorious for its bare rocks, hot sands
and rugged mountains, with only little vegetation. However,
in spite of such adverse conditions the people were able to
survive because the Lord had miraculously sustained them as
He had promised. During all this time the Lord was gracious
to His erring people, "They lacked nothing" said Nehemiah,
"their clothes waxed not old, and their feet swelled not". The
divine purpose in all this was that Israel might be taught to fear
God and walk in His ways, a purpose to an extent achieved
in the second generation, which had not rebelled in the same
high-handed manner as the ungrateful nation which was
rescued out of Egypt.

The Lord's care for His people in the wilderness is described
poetically in Psalm 105: "He spread a cloud for a covering;
and fire to give light in the night. They asked, and He brought
quails, and satisfied them with the bread of heaven. He opened
the rock, and waters gushed out". But Psalm 106 records the
ungrateful response: "They soon forgot His works; They
waited not for His counsel: But lusted exceedingly in the
wilderness, and tempted God in the desert".

There is much in similar vein recorded by Moses in his writings.
The burden Moses had to bear throughout those trying years

was a heavy one indeed. The desired haven of the promised land was near geographically, but its realization was deferred by frustrations and worries which followed one another in apparently never-ending succession, until at times Moses was almost in despair. Until Jordan was crossed there could be no relaxation or quiet enjoyment of the fruits of labour; the man of God must continue to endure patiently the foolishness and unbelief of his charges.

The apostle Paul had a similar experience as he nurtured the New Testament people of God. "Beside those things that are without", he said, "there is that which presseth upon me daily, anxiety for all the churches" (2 Corinthians 11:28). These great examples from Scripture teach that for those who try to serve the Lord, the delights of rest and relaxation are not to be sought in this life but must await the soon-coming day of reward.

As the forty years' journey began to draw to its close it seemed as though Moses' endurance would at last be rewarded, but with patience nearly exhausted and with another mutiny brewing at Meribah where there was no water, he momentarily failed and spoke angrily to the people. "He spake unadvisedly with his lips" (Psalm 106:33) so that God was not sanctified in the eyes of the children of Israel (Numbers 20:12). In his anxiety to quell the rebellion Moses committed a misdemeanour which might seem to be unimportant in human eyes, but to God it was of the utmost importance that His servant should reflect those gracious divine attributes which He consistently displayed towards Israel.

Moses should have addressed the people firmly but gently and with calm assurance, in full knowledge that the Lord was in control of the situation. How difficult! But God's righteousness must be publicly vindicated, and poor Moses, more sinned against than sinning, must bear the seemingly harsh punishment of exclusion from the land of promise. "It went ill with Moses for their sakes". After forty years of arduous and selfless service is he to receive nothing? There cannot be injustice with God; Moses' reward awaits a better, a happier day, when each man will receive his praise from God. Heavenly rewards are so much more to be prized than earthly ones.

The serious view taken in Scripture of the behaviour of the Israelites in the wilderness can be seen in the fact that the forty years is called "the provocation", for men provoked God time and time again and hardened their hearts against Him, therefore He said "I sware in My wrath, they shall not enter into My rest". It is sad to review such distasteful behaviour and its inevitable consequence of great blessings forfeited, but we can profit from past errors by observing carefully the lesson the writer of the letter to the Hebrews draws for us (chapters 3 and 4).

Our hearts can easily become like the Israelites, hardened by the deceitfulness of sin and full of unbelief. If we refuse to listen to the voice of the Lord speaking to us we may follow in the way of those whose carcasses fell in the wilderness. Unbelief is probably the sin the same writer had in mind when, after recounting the triumphs of faithful men and women, he says "Let us also ... lay aside every weight, and the sin which doth so easily beset us, and let us run with patience the race that is set before us" (Hebrews 12:1). Looking to ourselves, we must diligently avoid the errors of the wilderness murmurers so that we may experience the happiness of rest and fulfilment promised for the people of God under the New Covenant. This is not bodily rest, but a deep and satisfying rest of soul which accompanies steadfast service in God's house.

CHAPTER ELEVEN:
DEPARTURE (JOHN TERRELL)

———

Throughout Scripture we find repeatedly that the lasting fragrance of a life greatly used by God depends largely on the circumstances of its end. We need only compare Samson and Solomon to Joseph and Elijah to appreciate this point. It is among the lives whose fragrance lingers that Moses is found. Furthermore his end is one of those distinguished in the Word by unique dealings on the part of God with regard to the immediate circumstances of death. Not a miraculous translation as with Enoch or Elijah, but unusually tender funeral under the personal hand of his God, as we shall see.

Moses was a man of many words, few of them light or superfluous. A study has already been made in this book of Moses as the mediator of God's covenant with Israel at Sinai. There he became the bearer of divine utterances, received when in the presence of God on the mountain top. In this, as in many other respects, it is very easy to see parallels in the New Testament life and witness of Paul (see 2 Corinthians 12). It is clear, therefore, that we must give close attention to the closing words spoken by Moses to Israel before he died. So long as men and women are on the earth the last words of the loved and respected will be cherished. In a sense, the whole of the book of Deuteronomy is a last will and testament to the nation from their distinguished leader. The reiteration and elaboration of the principles of the law of God in this book were to remain a source book on the divine will for Israel for all time. Moses' concentrated earnestness in conveying these words to the people cannot have failed in its impact, and we readily appreciate the great weight of the words as we read them today.

Concentrating our attention for the present on the final chapters of Deuteronomy, we find in the opening words of chapter 29 that Moses appears to turn to a more personal address to the nation, having completed his main communication of "the covenant which the LORD commanded Moses to make with the children of Israel". In this chapter and in the following one Moses, the pleader with God, now pleads again with Israel. Many memorable words are uttered with passionate longing and holy zeal. Israel's marvellous heritage is summed up in Exodus 29:29 as "the things that are revealed belong to us and to our children forever". Moses was well aware that the language and message he transmitted were of no lesser stuff than divine revelation; disclosures from God according to His wisdom to whom "the secret things belong". This then was the true measure of Israel's responsibility and ours. Again our thoughts transfer to Paul and Timothy - a bequest of sound words and consequent solemn responsibility (2 Timothy 2:2). Again, we need hardly add the projection to our own day, and our responsibility is evident.

The language of the leader in Deuteronomy 30:1,15 is uncompromising, "the blessing and the curse"; "See, I have set before thee this day life and good, and death and evil". Yet mingled so tenderly with the binding solemnity of such warnings are the expressions of the longings of love. God's law respected and His word obeyed, "He", Moses declares, "will do thee good" (Exodus 30:5). Similar encouragements are found in the early verses of chapter 31 before the Lord once again speaks directly to His servant with dire forecast of national failure and a solemn charge concerning the song (v.19) which Moses in departing should teach Israel.

Deuteronomy 32:1-43 provides the text of this song. Studded with gems of poetic inspiration, this closing divine message through Moses is beyond the compass of this chapter for detailed comment: "My doctrine shall drop as the rain" (v.2). "The Rock, His work is perfect" (v.4). "For the LORD's portion is His people" (v.9). "Vengeance is Mine and recompense" (v.35). "I kill, and I make alive" (v.39). Longing and warning; loving ambition and fearful foreboding, mingled in touching pathos. The precious theme of "the Rock" arches far down the years to the words of the Spirit through Paul to the Corinthians, "and the Rock was Christ" (1 Corinthians 10:4).

But the beloved shepherd of God's people was to be permitted yet a few more personal words to his flock. "And this is the blessing, wherewith Moses the man of God blessed the children of Israel before his death" (Exodus 33:1). Again, no detailed treatment of this tender, prophetic benediction is possible here. The priestly things of Levi and the precious things of Joseph; the full blessing of Naphtali and strength for the day for Asher; all providing ample and rewarding ground for detailed study and meditation; all expressing a close perception and far-seeing vision on Moses' part in relation to the people he had loved and led. The appropriation of the words of Exodus 33:27 by millions of later generations who learned to love and trust Israel's God, would engender no grudge on Moses' part or that of Israel - "the eternal God is thy dwelling place, and underneath are the everlasting arms". Finally Moses' heart overflows, "Happy art thou, O Israel: who is like unto thee, a people saved by the LORD". The spiritual heritage of a New Testament people can be no less.

We turn briefly now to record two actions of Moses before he departed, and which he treated with a care which carries its lesson for us. Firstly, he both carefully recorded the words of the law of the Lord and ensured its preservation and sanctity. In Deuteronomy 31:24-26, we read of the completion of the writing, and the command to the Levites to "put it by the side of the ark of the covenant of the LORD your God". This recalls Samuel's later diligence in writing the manner of the kingdom and laying it up before the LORD (1 Samuel 10:25). There is much about the ark that speaks of Christ. The action of Moses underlines the inseparability of the Living Word and the written word.

With unerring spiritual insight, Moses knew the only possible source of success and prosperity for Israel. Secondly, Moses diligently prepared his successor. He carefully followed the Lord's instruction about Joshua's initiation into his approaching responsibilities, as indeed he had done from much earlier days. Exodus 31:7,8 admirably summarizes Moses' care in this matter, and a special personal word for Joshua was graciously added by the Lord in the solemn environment of the tent of meeting, "I will be with thee" (Exodus 31:23). Lesser men have been absorbed in their own departing glory but

Moses, like Paul with Timothy, proved a man of superior and selfless wisdom.

And so the last sunrise dawned on Mount Nebo for the Lord's ageing servant; and it was a divine hand with a tender touch which led him aloft. The terms in which the Lord repeated His righteous judgement on Moses for the failure of Meribah sound almost harsh to us. That such was not the tone of the words we can be sure, yet it seems that the abiding purpose of God in this matter must be repeated to Moses in quite unequivocal terms. God's honour was at stake and it is to Moses' eternal credit that no word of petulant pleading for himself escaped him. We may wonder whether he dared to hope in his own heart that his sentence might be commuted. What would be more human? Yet he doubtless understood with greater spiritual perception than we may often achieve, that God's word must stand and be reaffirmed. In this, his last selfless act of resignation to superior divine wisdom, Moses' spiritual and historical stature is immeasurably enhanced.

A strange ending honour, it may seem to us, that the hand of God Himself should secretly lay His servant to rest. Yet surely a touching and tender ministration, more honouring by far than punitive. "Them that honour Me I will honour". We need only glance at the many sayings of the Lord Jesus about Moses, and reflect on the glory of the transfiguration mount, to realize that here was the farewell of one of God's greatest servants. Eye undimmed and natural force unabated, the first full chapter of Moses' service closes. Holy Scripture bears ample witness to yet future distinction for the man "whom the LORD knew face to face".

CHAPTER TWELVE: SOME NEW TESTAMENT REFERENCES (FRED EVANS)

———

I f we had no Old Testament it would still be possible to construct a reasonably full account of the chronological events and the important characteristics of the life of Moses from the New Testament. There are almost sixty references to him, about half in the Gospels, the rest spread through the Acts of the Apostles and the Epistles, with one in the Revelation. The ground covers the period from his birth to his death and burial, with a possible glimpse of the future. The three forty-year phases of his life are dealt with, and various outstanding incidents are referred to in some detail. Space does not permit a consideration of many references, so it becomes necessary to select a few of them. Thus we propose to confine this chapter to specific exposition of some references in the Epistle to the Hebrews.

THE FAITH OF HIS PARENTS

Moses, "when he was born", was cradled in the faith of his godly parents. "They saw he was a goodly (KJV: proper) child". They apparently associated something with the child which caused them to feel that it was God's purpose to preserve and use him. It has even been suggested that they possibly had some divine revelation or word to rest on, which marked out the child as one through whom God designed to do a great work.

Their resultant faith caused them to hide the child for three months. Their faith triumphed over any fear they had - "they were not afraid of the king's commandment". They endangered their own lives to preserve the life of their child (Hebrews 11:23).

THE CHOICE OF FAITH

This example of personal parental faith found an answering response in their son, "when he was grown up". When he was ripe for mature deliberation, he was called on to make the vital decision. On the one hand, the princely status of a son of the daughter of the royal house of Pharaoh, with the remote possibility of eventually succeeding to the throne of Egypt. A life of enjoyment of all that Egypt had to offer in the way of treasures and pleasures, with the challenge of Egypt's progressive civilization and regal opportunity. On the other hand, identification with his own people, the Hebrews, a race of slaves. A life of suffering and self-denial, sharing their hardships and reproach. But a life with and for the people of God, with a divinely ordained destiny.

Moses was called to make this choice when he was forty years old, at a time when his powers of mind and body were fully developed. He had grown ripe for enjoyment, and at an age when he was capable of relishing material luxuries and the pleasant benefits which the world had to offer. It was no hasty impulse which guided him. But for him in these circumstances the pleasures of the world and the treasures of the court were 'the pleasures of sin". He refused them. He deliberately preferred to be known publicly as one with "the people of

God". He would not undervalue this true honour. These people might be a race of slaves, but to his faith they were God's chosen, "an elect race". The almighty God had:

HIS PURPOSES FOR THEM AND FOR HIM

What strengthened Moses in making his important and far-reaching decision? His faith in the Living God. And what motivated him? "He looked unto the recompense of reward". His eyes were turned away from the short-lived comfort and luxury: they were fixed on the eternal recompense (Hebrews 11:24-26).

FAITH IN THE INVISIBLE

In the pathway of faith one decision often leads on to others. Moses had made his choice - to involve himself with the people of God and to suffer evil treatment. It meant leaving his mother by adoption, and setting his back on the Egyptian court. But where was he to go? He could hardly expect any of the Hebrew slaves to hide him successfully. Could he conceal himself in the tawny-yellow desert lands flanking the river Nile or in the broad delta plains? Dare he leave the country entirely, so adding insult to injury, thus incurring the king's greater antagonism? Yes, this must be his course. "By faith he forsook Egypt: not fearing the wrath of the king". Dire consequences were likely to overtake him if he should be caught after leaving Egypt in defiance of Pharaoh.

He had resolved to play his part with the oppressed Israelites, which he could not have done satisfactorily if he had decided to remain. This motive constituted his act of faith, "for he endured, as seeing Him who is invisible". His dealings were with God alone, who though invisible to his bodily eyes was ever before his "eyes of faith" (Hebrews 11:27).

THE VISION OF FAITH

The next step of faith in the life of Moses taken up by the Holy Spirit in Hebrews 11 is of rather a different nature yet a vital link in the chain. "By faith he kept (instituted) the passover, and the sprinkling of the blood, that the destroyer of the firstborn should not touch them" (v.28).

By this time Moses was quite aware of the role he was expected by God to fulfil in His purposes for His people. God had promised that the destroyer would pass over and not touch the occupiers of the blood-sprinkled houses. Moses believed God and rested on the promise. As Calvin wrote, "He acquiesced in the bare word of God where the thing itself was not apparent". His faith also helped the people to believe beforehand in the certainty of divine judgement upon the firstborn of Egypt and of divine shelter for Israel complying with the appointed provision of the sprinkled blood. But his faith went further than that.

Of the Passover, the LORD had said, "Ye shall keep it a feast to the LORD: throughout your generations ye shall keep it a feast by an ordinance for ever" (Exodus 12:14). Moses again believed God and "instituted" the feast. Is it too much to suggest that faith's vision which Moses saw for his enslaved people was of a free. united and obedient people, established in a national home, regularly keeping the Passover for centuries to come? They would remember their emancipation from Egypt and their divine Emancipator in the manner of his instituting. Fifteen centuries later, the Messiah Himself was to say, "With desire I have desired to eat this passover with you before I suffer" (Luke 22:15). It was on this occasion that the Lord Jesus instituted a different memorial for His New Testament people when He said, "This do in remembrance of Me".

MOSES AND FAITHFULNESS

The true man of faith becomes a faithful man. The two Greek words are from the same root. The person who truly believes or has a firm persuasion becomes one on whom reliance can be placed. He is worthy of trust or trustworthy and reliable. This was true of Moses - in all God's house he was faithful to God who appointed him as His servant. "My servant Moses ... is faithful in all Mine house" (Numbers 12:7). This was not man's testimony but that of the all-seeing and almighty God. It was and still is the witness of the only One who had complete knowledge of Moses - his character, his motives and his actions. A wonderful testimony indeed! It was spoken at the door of "the tent of meeting".

The earlier word to Moses had been emphatic and clear: "Let them make Me a sanctuary; that I may dwell among them. According to all that I show thee, the pattern of the tabernacle, and the pattern of all the furniture thereof, even so shall ye make it" (Exodus 25:8,9).

There was to be no introduction by Moses of any of his own ideas based on a close connection with the constructions and traditions of Egypt. Neither were there to be any modifications according to his own personal whims. The pattern had been shown him in the Mount. The actual construction of the Tabernacle and all its contents was faithfully executed under Moses' supervision according to God's pattern. Its erection and the detailed arrangements for its consecration, also administrative arrangements connected with the High Priest and the supporting priests, with their consecration - everything was done "as the LORD commanded Moses". With this faithfulness the great Jehovah God was so satisfied that "the cloud covered the tent of meeting, and the glory of the LORD filled the tabernacle" (Exodus 40:34). This was an outstanding day in the life of Moses and the people of God. The day of fulfilled desire on the part of the LORD God when He in His glory had actually come to dwell among His people. It was also a day of triumph of faith and faithfulness on the part of Moses, His meek and honoured servant.

"For Moses: he forsook the land

Where wealth and power were in his hand:

By faith the passover he kept,

Led Israel forth while Rahab wept:

We give Thee thanks."

CHAPTER THIRTEEN: MOSES THE GENTLEMAN (JOHN MILLER)

When God chose a leader for the people of Israel He chose a gentleman in the true meaning of this word, for "the man Moses was very meek, above all the men which were upon the face of the earth".

Moses' character was quite the reverse of Jehu's. There was nothing of gentleness in Jehu. When the watchman upon the tower of Jezreel saw him approach, he spoke of his driving as being "like the driving of Jehu the son of Nimshi; for he driveth furiously". Jehu was suited for the work for which he was chosen - to execute God's vengeance upon the house of Ahab, but though he swept away Ahab's vile house it did not bring him one bit nearer God; for "Jehu took no heed to walk in the law of the Lord, the God of Israel, with all his heart: he departed not from the sins of Jeroboam, wherewith he made Israel to sin" (2 Kings 10:31).

Moses, accustomed to follow the flock of Jethro his father-in-law, was of a meek, gentle disposition, and he would have been content to have lived out his life in quietness in such pastoral scenes (Exodus 2:21) but God had chosen him to lead a greater flock (Psalm 77:20; Isaiah 63:11). Moses was gentle towards men, not easily offended, and bore patiently as a nursing father the murmurings and ill-behaviour of the people of Israel, but he was unyielding and unbending when it was a question of obedience to the Word of God - "Moses indeed was faithful in all His [God's] house as a servant" (Hebrews 3:5). Jehu was quite the reverse of Moses towards men he showed no gentleness, and towards God no faithfulness, for, as we have seen, he took no heed to walk in the law of the Lord.

As we write, we think of that perfectly meek and gentle Man, our blessed Lord, who said: "I am meek and lowly in heart", who at the end of His lowly life was led as a gentle lamb to the slaughter. When He was reviled, He reviled not again, and when He suffered, threatened not. He committed His cause to God, and though condemned by men could say in the words through Isaiah - "He is near that justifieth Me" (Isaiah 50:8). If we but followed more closely in His ways how much of sorrow we would save both ourselves and others! If the coals of fire, of which Paul writes in Romans 12:20, were more often used we would, no doubt, all be a great deal warmer.

CHAPTER FOURTEEN: CONCLUDING REVIEW (TOM HYLAND)

———

How do we measure true greatness? Secular history has passed its verdict on men and women in many spheres of human endeavour. The famous and the infamous have been scrutinized and appraised. In modern times there has been a vogue to rewrite history, to overturn earlier assessments and to debunk many of those who were acclaimed and idolized in former ages.

To be truthful, human judgement is no criterion in such matters. In their assessments of men and events, historians, ancient and modern, are seldom impartial. True greatness is not assessed at the bar of history. God alone is the Judge. And it is one of the marks of the truly great that they do not court publicity nor pander to human opinion. Thus Paul, the apostle, fully aware of the whisperings of his critics, wrote: "But with me it is a very small thing that I should be judged of you, or of man's judgement: ... He that judgeth me is the Lord" (1 Corinthians 4:3,4).

Scripture biographies are in a class apart; character is disclosed without distortion, failures and triumphs are recorded without partiality. Men are measured, not by the fame they have brought to themselves but by the place they have filled in the unfolding purpose of God. In every age God has employed human instrumentality to further His great designs.

In his address in the synagogue at Antioch of Pisidia Paul summed up the lifework of one of God's great men in one concise phrase: "David, after he had in his own generation served the counsel of God, fell on sleep" (Acts 13:36). David "served the counsel of God": so did Moses, so did Paul, and many another in his own generation. In the great day of disclosure the record will bring to light the full story, "And each true-hearted servant shall shine as doth the day."

In this book, we have reviewed the Scripture record of a great man of God, and have reflected on some of the lessons to be learned from it. The name of Moses, "the servant of the LORD", occupies a unique place in the unfolding story of redemption. For nearly four hundred years God had waited for the seed of Abraham to develop into a disciplined, virile people. The miracle of their preservation under divine providence, from the call of Abraham to their enslavement in Egypt, is graphically described in Psalm 105. When the time came for God to move forward to the next stage of his saving purpose a leader was needed, and Moses was at hand prepared and ready for the task. Then, "He sent Moses His servant, and Aaron whom He had chosen" and "He brought them forth. And there was not one feeble person among His tribes. And He brought forth His people with joy, And His chosen with singing" (Psalm 105:26,37,43).

Our writers have highlighted the various stages in the preparation and training of God's servant. In this closing chapter, we underline some of the salient points.

The narrative of the family history of Moses begins, "There went a man of the house of Levi, and took to wife a daughter of Levi" (Exodus 2:1); a commonplace statement, maybe, but by no means a commonplace event. A godly marriage holds great spiritual potential. This was not a favourable time to rear a family. Amram and Jochebed's third child was born under the sentence of death. Mothers were casting out their babies at the command of a ruthless tyrant. No other course seemed possible. But Moses' parents were sustained by a faith which does not adjust to circumstances. God honoured that faith and brought back to them their "goodly child" from the very jaws of death. In their godly Hebrew home Amram and Jochebed were entrusted with the early training of God's chosen leader. The time was short; the task was urgent. The result was decisive. When Moses left the slave dwelling for the palace splendour the groundwork of his character had been well and truly laid. That early training would bear abundant fruit.

The mother of Charles and John Wesley was asked, "How soon do you begin to train your children?" She replied, "I begin six months before they are born". By self-discipline and self-sacrifice she enriched her offspring and served her generation. The life of Moses was an ordered life. It is presented in Scripture in three forty-year periods. Each of these periods has been reviewed in this book. The first was complete when Moses "went out unto his brethren, and looked on their burdens" (Exodus 2:11). That was a day of destiny in the overall plan of his training. The smiting of the Egyptian was no mere impetuous flash of temper. In his heart he had already renounced Egypt and cast in his lot with his persecuted brethren. Calmly and deliberately he had weighed in the balances the treasures of Egypt and the "reproach of Christ". As the son of Pharaoh's daughter an illustrious future, by worldly standards, beckoned him. His character, his gifts and his training fitted him for high office among the statesmen of his age. But to Moses came the vision of the true riches; riches of a sort which would endure when Egypt's tinsel glory had faded into oblivion.

Egypt's treasures had been produced by the lash of the taskmaster, by merciless oppression. In contrast the true wealth, the pursuit of which would now captivate his heart and dominate his life, could be acquired only by renunciation, rejection and reproach. Moses saw from afar the vision of the Christ who by these means would endow men with His "unsearchable riches". Then he made his memorable choice, a choice which would have its sequel centuries later when on the Mount of Transfiguration he would be given the high honour of conversing with the rejected Christ.

In every age the challenge of these two ways of life has been presented to men of God in the making. Some, like Moses, have taken the one path, others, like Demas, have taken the other. Momentous decision! Today, as ever, aspiring men and women of God must choose. There is no middle path. The Master Himself put the issues clearly to His followers: "Whosoever would save his life shall lose it: and whosoever shall lose his life for My sake shall find it" (Matthew 16:25).

Moses fled from the palace with the pain of rejection in his heart. His resolve to identify himself with his persecuted brethren had been angrily rebuffed. To strike an Egyptian was one thing, it was quite another to reconcile two contentious brethren. They resented his interference in their private quarrel. He thought they would understand his concern and he expected them to respond to his counsel. Hadn't they enough trouble without the scourge of personal antagonism? That day Moses learned the early lesson that those he was called to serve had all the latent perversity of sinful human nature which even the iron furnace of Egypt could not eradicate. If Moses was to lead this people he would require far more than mere human wisdom. And he was not yet ready for such a formidable task. The palace education was valuable and necessary but it was not enough. To complete his training the forty years in the Egyptian court must be followed by a forty-year sojourn in the wilderness. This was the environment in which his service to God's people would be discharged. The solitude and austerity of the wilderness would provide conditions in which the necessary spiritual qualities could be assimilated into his character. Thus it was arranged in the divine plan.

The experience of Moses gives the answer to many questions which arise in the development of men and women of God. There is no need for us to question, Why this or why that? God knows the end from the beginning. Reverses and seeming setbacks can only be judged by the results they produce. God prepares and disposes of His servants according to His own will. He has His men in hiding and brings them to their tasks in His own time.

In chapter two, I commented on the sudden call to service which came to Moses at the burning bush. That encounter with God was not only the signal for Moses to begin his life-work. It was also a decisive step forward in the revelation of the Divine Being. The disclosure of the Divine Name and the infinite grace of the eternal I AM in encouraging His reluctant servant are among the things written aforetime "for our learning". One of the lessons to be learned from that incident is that God never calls to a task without supplying the necessary grace to perform it.

The record of Israel's journey from Egypt to Canaan is an epic in Bible history. The narrative is a source-book of instruction in the ways of God. Israel's redemption by blood and by power, the Red Sea crossing, the historic covenant at Sinai, manna from heaven, water from the smitten rock, and the construction of a dwelling-place for God in the wilderness are landmarks in the dealings of God with men.

But if the narrative is full of instruction in the ways of God it also exposes the inborn depravity of the human heart. The base ingratitude of this favoured people, their persistent murmuring and their unbelief culminating in the disastrous rebellion at Kadesh-barnea, make depressing reading. The trek across the desert with this great multitude would have been trying enough even if the people had been loyal and co-operative. They were not. Sorrowfully, in one brief sentence, Moses summed up his forty years' travail with them: "Ye have been rebellious against the LORD from the day that I knew you" (Deuteronomy 9:24). And the divine verdict on this epoch in Israel's history is no less severe: "Forty years long was I grieved with that generation, And said, It is a people that do err in their heart, And they have not known My ways: Wherefore I sware in My wrath, That they should not enter into My rest" (Psalm 95:10-11).

At the beginning, we enquired, "How do we measure true greatness?" Here is one feature of Moses' life and work which bears the hall-mark of the man of God. In spite of the heartbreak this people brought him, he harboured no resentment, he indulged in no self-pity. He endured their ruthless hostility and their pitiless abuse; "They be almost ready to stone me" (Exodus 17:4), he lamented on one occasion. He refused to cower to their threats, yet he pleaded their cause and stood in the breach when the anger of the Lord waxed hot against them. Sadly, as the Lord instructed him, he led them back from Kadesh-barnea.

The generation he had brought from Egypt would die in the wilderness, but Moses was prepared to serve them until their children were ready to possess the promised land. What a man! What a leader! Such selfless devotion to his allotted task finds an echo in the words of a great New Covenant leader, the apostle Paul. The Corinthian church was his "work in the Lord" (1 Corinthians 9:1). He was not well treated by them. Yet, although longing for their responding love, he bore no grudge, "I seek not yours, but you", he wrote, "I will most gladly spend and be spent for your souls" (2 Corinthians 12:14,15). There is real greatness, the insignia of the true servant of Christ.

We now refer briefly to another important aspect of Moses' service to God and to mankind. He was not only the distinguished desert leader, he was also chosen by the Spirit of God to record the early history of man, the biographies of the patriarchs and the formation of the nation of Israel. His work in this field was monumental. The first five books of Scripture are the cornerstone of divine revelation. Their authorship, often disputed by critics, is settled once for all by the testimony of the Lord Jesus. He described the Pentateuch as "the book of Moses" (Mark 12:26), and quoted from each of its five parts, thus setting His seal upon their divine authority. Borne along by the Holy Spirit the first of the great prophets of the Old Covenant bequeathed to us many precious foreshadowings of the Coming One; "the sufferings of the Christ, and the glories that should follow them" receiving ample treatment in type and parable, as well as in direct prophecy. Man of vision! Looking down the ages he penned the assuring oracle: "The Lord your God will raise up for you a Prophet like me from your brethren. Him you shall hear in all things, whatever He says to you" (Acts 3:22 NKJV).

In chapter nine, Laurie gave us a graphic account of closing days of this eminent man of God. With eye undimmed, natural force unabated, the great prophet of the desert ascended Mount Pisgah to view the land "flowing with milk and honey". By divine chastisement and for dispensational reasons he would not be allowed to enter it. There it was, stretched out before him, from the Jordan valley to the green uplands of Galilee. He drank in the picture. It was just as God had promised. The aged pilgrim envisaged the people he loved and served settled in their tribal inheritances in Immanuel's land. Touching moment! Then with measured step he descended to the plain of Moab and his God wrote 'finis' to the earthly sojourn of His devoted servant. His mortal frame was committed to the desert sands. His tomb was secret, no pillar marked the spot. But his never-to-be-forgotten exploits are indelibly inscribed in the eternal record.